MAHATMA GANDHI
AND THE BAHÁ'ÍS

Mahatma Gandhi
and the Bahá'ís

Striving Towards a
Non-violent Civilization

M. V. Gandhimohan

Universidade Federal de Alagoas

Bahá'í Publishing Trust
New Delhi, India

First Edition: August 2000

ISBN: 81-86953-82-5

Cover art by Gail Jennings

Published by the Bahá'í Publishing Trust,
F-3/6, Okhla Industrial Area, Phase-I, New Delhi, India

Printed by Rakmo Press (P) Ltd., New Delhi

To my parents,
To my family,
To humankind.

Preface

Many of Gandhi's teachings are remarkably similar to those of the Bahá'í Faith. This book attempts to compare their religious, ethical, and socioeconomic teachings, and I hope that it will contribute to increase dialogue and cooperation between the Bahá'ís and the community of Gandhi's followers and admirers worldwide. This work also represents my personal expression of deep thanks to Gandhi, on the occasion of the fiftieth anniversary of the culmination of his life of service—and ultimate sacrifice—in 1948, when he departed his earthly life with God's mention on his lips.

Gandhi was born on 2 October 1869, and I was born during his one hundredth birth anniversary. To commemorate the occasion, my parents named me Gandhimohan, meaning Gandhi-admirer. As a child I was deeply influenced by Gandhi through my parents' adherence to many of his ethical and moral teachings.

My association with the Bahá'í Faith began when I was a teenager. I learned then about the Bahá'í belief that the major world religions are different parts of a single progressive process of divine revelation. To me, the idea that all faiths have a divine origin and purpose resonated very well with Gandhi's teachings that Religion, like Truth, is One. Subsequently I joined the Bahá'í community.

The reader deserves to know something about my qualifications for writing this book. I am not a scholar of religion, nor am I trained in the humanities, but rather my training is in theoretical physics. My background in statistical physics, which deals with macroscopic phenomena that emerge from the interaction of many microscopic components, shapes to some extent my understanding of social, economic, political, and historical processes. I thus very briefly discuss this point here, since it may be of interest to the reader. When a substance approaches a phase transition, such as the change of state from solid ice to liquid water, local fluctuations (of say, density) grow until a "critical state" is reached. Near this critical point, fluctuations in every part of the system become "correlated," no matter how great the distance between them, and the system appears "fractal." As the phase transition continues past the critical point, the correlations become weaker again and finally the entire system changes over to the new ordered state. The ideas that emerged in the 1960's and 70's from the study of phase transitions eventually found application not only in related fields of physics, but also in other sciences, such as cardiology and economics. To a significant extent, such ideas also influenced my personal understanding of the transition process from the old world order, organized along the lines of "sovereign" and "independent" nations, to the new World Order foretold and described by Bahá'u'lláh, a spiritual civilization ordered and governed globally through interdependent institutions of planetary scope. In this book, I try to show that the moral, political, and social writings of both Gandhi and the Bahá'ís point to a deeply spiritual collective future for our planet. Ours is the privilege—and duty—to help complete this transition to the emerging World Order.

I have refrained from using the title "Mahatma" (great spirit) because I feel that Gandhi may have disliked it were he alive today.* His statements regarding his distaste for lofty titles include the following: "My Mahatmaship is worthless." "I hold it to be a blasphemy to represent me as Shri Krishna." "I have become literally sick of the adoration of the unthinking multitude." "Though a non-co-operator, I shall gladly subscribe to a Bill to make it criminal for anybody to call me Mahatma and to touch my feet. Where I can impose the law myself, i.e., at the Ashram, the practice is criminal." "Truth to me is infinitely dearer than the 'mahatmaship', which is purely a burden."†

Please note that the views expressed in this book do not in any way represent authoritative Bahá'í doctrine, but rather my own personal understanding of the subject matter. Indeed, the Bahá'í Faith has no equivalent of clergy and teaches that each person is duty-bound to seek truth independently of others, especially when relating to religious, social, economic or political matters.

January 1998
Natal, Brazil

M. V. Gandhimohan

---

*The book title is one notable exception.
†Quoted from *The Mind of Mahatma Gandhi*.

Acknowledgements

This book, though written by me, owes its existence to many others. Many people have helped directly, and countless others have contributed indirectly, perhaps without even being aware of it. I thus feel that it is impossible for me to express my gratitude adequately to all of them, nevertheless I wish to thank explicitly those who come to the forefront of my mind.

First, I thank those people who were directly involved in helping me write. I wish to acknowledge my deep thanks to Dr. Robert Stockman, without whose advice, encouragement, and feedback I would never have undertaken to write this book. I thank the National Spiritual Assembly of the Bahá'ís of India for very helpful comments. I thank the staff of the Office of External Affairs of the National Spiritual Assembly of the Bahá'ís of India, and Dr. A. K. Merchant in particular, for providing extremely helpful historical information regarding Gandhi's contacts with the Bahá'ís. I thank Anil Sarwal and R. N. Shah for being so encouraging and for very helpful suggestions. I thank J. Doostdar, N. Doostdar, G. Kingdon, R. Kingdon and L. Yancy for help with early versions of Section 1.1 when it was still in the form of a pamphlet. To Jiten Mishra and the staff of the Bahá'í Publishing Trust of India I express my sincere thanks for their help. I thank Mark Towfiq, Mark Jolly and Cyrus Monadjemi for very inspiring discussions. I thank Robert W. Nowak for help at various stages of the manuscript and for the fantastic proof-reading.

I also express my deep thanks to my parents, Uma Viswanathan and Dr. Tenkasi Muthukrisha Viswanathan, who instilled me with spiritual values from childhood. I thank them especially for educating me about nonviolence and teaching me about Gandhi, as well as for proofreading the manuscript. I thank my brother M. V. Dhuruvan for his moral support. I thank my mother-in-law Gail Jennings for excellent feedback. I thank my wife, Heather Dea Jennings, for her in-depth critical evaluation, her excellent support, and her extensive proof-reading of the manuscript.

I also take the liberty, perhaps a little unusual, of thanking the creators of the free software I used to write this book. This book was written using the TeX and LaTeX typesetting software using the GNU Emacs editor, often on systems running Linux. Aside from being among the best such software available at the time of writing, they are also completely free, consistent with the Gandhian ideal that intellectual property should be for the common good of all, rather than for the private gain of a small elite.

Finally, I thank God.

Contents

Chapter 1

Introduction

Humans have an innate tendency to strive for truth as rational beings, and to strive for justice as social and political beings. Civilization results. But once in about a thousand years, the structure of social organization changes. History is punctuated at odd times by critical events whose revolutionary effects set them apart as the reference points by which we relate to our collective past. Such critical periods include, for example, the agricultural revolution, the emergence of city states, and the rise of nations and empires. Social life before and after such landmark events is markedly different, because there occurs a shift in the constellation of forces which govern the state of affairs. Indeed, each of these moments marks the closing of an aeon and the opening of another—old patterns give way to new ones. The ensuing vortices of transformation leave no aspect of life unchanged. Today, there are ample signs that the world is undergoing another period of major transformation. An old world order is passing away—and a new one emerging—before our very eyes.

Until the 18th century, the world was organized as separate and effectively independent sovereign nation states. Nations conquered nations, and mighty religions waged devastating "holy" wars. The earth was still to a large extent a flat, infinite plane, so that land and natural resources could be assumed to be inexhaustible. Exponential growth in riches and power was thus possible in some cases, a prized ideal indeed. Now, on the other hand, the situation is markedly different. National sovereignty today is a relic of the past. Which nation state today can be said to be fully sovereign? Indeed, nations today are more interdependent than independent. There have been corresponding, parallel changes occurring at practically every level of human society. Completely new economic processes have emerged, and sometimes frustrate attempts to sustain stable growth. The interconnectivity and complexity of the world are daily increasing, driven in part by breath-taking scientific and technological advances and their corollary effects on other facets of human civilization. Interestingly, this radical transformation in human life has begun to affect the entire planet. Greenhouse gases generated by human activity, and global warming, for example, can affect entire ecosystems—nay rather the entire biosphere. The earth is becoming a smaller, different place: so different, in fact, that many current social problems have no historical precedent. Humankind stands at a crossroads.

We now have a fresh opportunity to benefit from a critical reexamination of the principles that guide our individual and collective lives. Already, our rapidly changing world is searching for new human values, new guiding principles. The ideologies of the past are struggling to stay relevant: nationalism, ethnocentrism, racism, religious fundamentalism, partisan politics, sexism and radical feminism, atheism, consumerism, materialism, communism, supremacist theories, etc. are, one and all, being questioned. People everywhere appear to be awakening to the possibility that a new, *nonviolent,* approach to civilization is possible: one based on human values. Specifically, we are struggling to find levels of knowledge and modes of behavior that are consistent with the world's current condition.

In this context, this book presents some of the more pertinent teachings of Mohandas Karamchand Gandhi and of the Bahá'í Faith, arguably two of the more important agents that have contributed to the shaping of human society since their birth in the 19th century and that continue to influence people's thinking today. The reader of this book will note many striking similarities between the worldview of Gandhi and that of the Bahá'ís. Accordingly, most of the following chapters focus on the similarities in their thinking. There are, however, a handful of important differences between the Gandhian and the Bahá'í viewpoints that cannot be dismissed. Hence one chapter is devoted entirely to examining these major differences.

Some effort has been made in most chapters to present Gandhian and Bahá'í perspectives on an equal footing, in order to render this book as objective and impartial as may be possible. Such an unbiased approach has obvious advantages, but may inadvertently send the wrong message to some readers. A casual reader, for example, may get the (false) impression that the Bahá'í Faith is equal, on many levels, to the philosophy of Gandhi. A majority of Gandhi's admirers worldwide are not Bahá'ís; similarly not all Bahá'ís may know exactly who Gandhi was or what he did. Hence, such points need to be addressed explicitly from the very outset. The core question relates to what Gandhi and the Bahá'ís believe about their respective teachings. Gandhi claimed to be a free thinker and an ardent seeker of truth, but he never made claims to any kind of special divine authority. Most importantly, Gandhi did not set out to start a new religion. In contrast, the Bahá'í Faith is an organized world religion that Bahá'ís believe is an independent divine revelation. This major difference between the Gandhian and Bahá'í perspectives tinges, to however small an extent, virtually every other consideration of the subject matter. Hence, it is not altogether inconceivable that comparing Gandhian and Bahá'í teachings may be as inappropriate as comparing apples and oranges. And yet such comparisons need not be fruitless—e.g., are not both apples and oranges sweet?

This short book could never represent a comprehensive treatment of the subject matter, for the collected works of Gandhi comprise 90 volumes, while the writings of Bahá'u'lláh, the prophet-founder of the Bahá'í Faith, alone number over 100 volumes. For more information about the Bahá'í Faith, the reader is first referred to John E. Esslemont's classic textbook on the subject.[1] For more information about Gandhi, the reader is referred to any of the very good books about him, e.g., by Raghavan Iyer and Eknath Easwaran.[2-4] The next few pages briefly introduce the reader to the basic history and teachings of the Bahá'ís and of M. K. Gandhi.

1.1   The Bahá'í Faith

Early History

Bahá'u'lláh, the prophet-founder of the Bahá'í Faith, was born Husayn-'Alí in Persia on 12 November 1817—about 52 years before Gandhi. His aristocratic family could trace its ancestry back to the great dynasties of Persia's imperial past, as well as claim descent from the biblical Abraham. Declining the ministerial career open to him in government, he chose instead to devote his energies to a range of philanthropies which had, by the early 1840's, earned him widespread renown as "Father of the Poor." This privileged existence swiftly eroded after 1844, when Bahá'u'lláh became one of the leading advocates of a movement that was destined to change the course of his country's history.

In 1844 a young merchant from the city of Shiraz, known to history as the Báb, announced that the Day of God was at hand, and that he was the One promised in Islamic scripture. Although himself the bearer of an independent revelation from God, the Báb declared that his mission was to prepare mankind for the advent of that universal Messenger of God, "He Whom God will make manifest," awaited by the followers of all religions. The claim evoked violent hostility from the Muslim clergy, who taught that the process of Divine Revelation had ended with Muhammad and that any assertion to the contrary represented apostasy, punishable by death. Some 20 000 followers of the new faith were massacred throughout the country, and the Báb was publicly executed in 1850. Bahá'u'lláh was arrested for his prominence in defending the message of the Báb. He was then made to endure forty years of exile, imprisonment, and bitter persecution. Confiscating his wealth and properties, the Persian authorities banished Bahá'u'lláh to Baghdad.

The Bahá'í Faith was born in Baghdad in 1863, when Bahá'u'lláh declared to a number of his companions that he was the One promised by the Báb. Bahá'u'lláh in Arabic means the "Glory of God." He preached that the "earth is but on country, and mankind its citizens." He claimed to be a Manifestation of the attributes of God, and repeatedly identified himself with being the Promised One of all ages: Christ returned "in the glory of the Father" to Christendom, the Lord of Hosts to the Jews, Mihdí to the Muslims, Kalki Avatar to the Hindus, the Fifth Buddha to the Buddhists, and Sháh-Bahrám to the Zoroastrians. After being banished to Constantinople and Adrianople, Bahá'u'lláh was finally exiled to 'Akká in the Holy Land, where he died of natural causes in 1892. Bahá'u'lláh was succeeded by his son 'Abdu'l-Bahá (1844–1921) as the Head of the Faith, and subsequently by Shoghi Effendi (1897–1957), Bahá'u'lláh's great-grandson and Guardian of the Bahá'í Faith.

Bahá'í Teachings

Beginning in September 1867, Bahá'u'lláh wrote a series of letters to world leaders such as Emperor Napoleon III, Queen Victoria, Kaiser Wilhelm I, Tsar Alexander II of Russia, Emperor Franz Joseph, Pope Pius IX, Sultán 'Abdu'l-'Azíz of the Ottoman Empire, and the Persian ruler Násiri'd-Dín Sháh, among others. They dismissed his message. Today, in contrast, Bahá'u'lláh's vision of humanity as one people and of the earth as a common homeland stands vindicated. Indeed, it has become the focus of human hope. Bahá'u'lláh has left to posterity over a hundred volumes of written works. The original texts have been meticulously preserved, and the central body of these writings has been translated into more than eight hundred languages.[5] Bahá'ís consider these texts to be holy scripture.

Bahá'u'lláh's teachings proclaim the oneness of God, the oneness of humankind,[*] and the oneness of religion.[†] The central teachings of the Bahá'í Faith all stem from the concept of unity and include the following:

• Independent Investigation of the Truth

Bahá'u'lláh teaches that a fundamental obligation of human beings is to acquire knowledge with their "own eyes and not through the eyes of others."[6] A major cause of conflict in the world today is the fact that many people blindly and uncritically subscribe

---

[*]See also Chapter 6.
[†]See also Chapter 3.

to various traditions, movements, and opinions. Bahá'ís believe
that each human being has the capacity to differentiate truth from
falsehood. If people fail to use their intellect and choose instead
to accept without question certain opinions and ideas, either out
of admiration for or fear of those who uphold them, then they are
neglecting their basic moral responsibility as rational human beings. Moreover, when people act in this way, they often become
attached to some particular opinion or tradition, and thus intol-
erant of those who differ. Such emotional attachment can lead to
conflict. History has witnessed conflict and even bloodshed over
slight alterations in religious practice, or a minor change in the interpretation of doctrine. Personal search for truth enables people
to know why they adhere to a given ideology or doctrine.

• **Harmony of Science and Religion**

Bahá'u'lláh teaches that there can be no conflict between true science and true religion. 'Abdu'l-Bahá explains that science and religion operate in mutually complementary spheres: "Religion and
science are the two wings upon which man's intelligence can soar
into the heights... It is not possible to fly with one wing alone!
Should a man try to fly with the wing of religion alone he would
quickly fall into the quagmire of superstition, whilst on the other
hand, with the wing of science alone he would... fall into the de-
spairing slough of materialism."[7]

• **Progressive Revelation**

Referring to the various independent world religions, Bahá'u'lláh
writes: "These principles and laws, these firmly-established and
mighty systems, have proceeded from one Source, and are the rays
of one Light. That they differ one from another is to be attributed
to the varying requirements of the ages in which they were promulgated."[8] Religious revelation is progressive, not final.*

• **Emancipation of Women**

Bahá'í s believe that permanent international peace is unattainable unless and until women are welcomed into full partnership in

---

*See also Section 3.5.

all fields of human endeavor. 'Abdu'l-Bahá explains: "Humanity is like a bird with its two wings—the one is male, the other female. Unless both wings are strong and impelled by some common force, the bird cannot fly heavenwards..."[9] "The world in the past has been ruled by force, and man has dominated over woman by reason of his more forceful and aggressive qualities both of body and mind. But the balance is already shifting; force is losing its dominance, and mental alertness, intuition, and the spiritual qualities of love and service, in which woman is strong, are gaining ascendancy. Hence the new age will be an age less masculine and more permeated with the feminine ideals, or, to speak more exactly, will be an age in which the masculine and feminine elements of civilization will be more evenly balanced."[10]

• Universal Education

Bahá'u'lláh teaches that all children must be educated. He explains: "Man is the supreme Talisman. Lack of a proper education hath, however, deprived him of that which he doth inherently possess... Regard man as a mine rich in gems of inestimable value. Education can, alone, cause it to reveal its treasures, and enable mankind to benefit therefrom."[11] Bahá'í s give priority to the education of women and girls, since it is through educated mothers that the benefits of knowledge can be most effectively and rapidly diffused throughout society. Bahá'í s also believe that teaching the concept of world citizenship should be an important part of the education of every child.

• Extremes of Poverty and Wealth

Bahá'u'lláh calls for the elimination of the inordinate disparity between rich and poor. Although social laws are necessary for the regulation of wealth, the economic problems are essentially spiritual in origin. Bahá'u'lláh writes: "O Ye Rich Ones on Earth! The poor in your midst are My trust; guard ye My trust, and be not intent only on your own ease."[12]

• Abandonment of Prejudice

All forms of prejudice must be abandoned, including religious strife, unbridled nationalism, and racism. Bahá'u'lláh is unequivocal in these matters: "Consort with the followers of all religions in a spirit of friendliness and fellowship... It is not his to boast who loveth his country, but it is his who loveth the world."[13] As to racism, its practice perpetrates too outrageous a violation of the dignity of human beings to be countenanced under any pretext. 'Abdu'l-Bahá explains: "Concerning the prejudice of race: it is an illusion, a superstition pure and simple! For God created us all of one race... Why should man invent such a prejudice?"[14]

• Universal Auxiliary Language

Bahá'u'lláh calls for a world language. A fundamental lack of communication between peoples seriously undermines efforts towards world order. The adoption of an international language, to be taught as a second language in all schools, would go far towards resolving this problem and deserves urgent attention.

• A World Commonwealth

Shoghi Effendi wrote as far back as in 1936: "Unification of the whole of mankind is the hall-mark of the stage which human society is now approaching. Unity of family, of tribe, of city-state, and nation have been successively attempted and fully established. World unity is the goal towards which a harassed humanity is striving. Nation-building has come to an end. The anarchy inherent in state sovereignty is moving towards a climax. A world, growing to maturity, must abandon this fetish, recognize the oneness and wholeness of human relationships, and establish once for all the machinery that can best incarnate this fundamental principle of its life."[15]

The Bahá'í Community

Already in 1992, Encyclopedia Britannica Book of the Year indicated that the Bahá'í Faith is the most widely diffused religion on earth after Christianity. The Bahá'í community numbers more than six million members, and there are now Bahá'ís in every country on earth. Over 2100 nationalities and tribes are represented.

Bahá'í s give great importance to community life. All administrative authority is vested in elected institutions at the local, national, and international levels. There is no ritual, no clergy. The supreme ruling body of the Bahá'í Faith is the Universal House of Justice, located in Haifa, Israel. It was first elected in 1963 in what probably was the first global, truly democratic election in the history of our planet. Since then, the community has initiated and has been actively engaged in thousands of social and economic development projects in many parts of the world.

Believing that the United Nations represents a major effort in the unification of the planet, Bahá'ís strive to support its work in every way possible. The Bahá'í International Community is accredited with consultative status with the United Nations Economic and Social Council (ECOSOC) and with the United Nations Children's Fund (UNICEF). The Bahá'í Community's offices in New York and Geneva and Bahá'ís in many lands regularly participate in conferences, congresses and seminars concerned with the socio-economic life of our planet.

1.2   M. K. Gandhi

Biographical Sketch

Mohandas Karamchand Gandhi was born on 2 October 1869 in Porbandar, India—at a time when Bahá'u'lláh had been exiled to the Holy Land as a prisoner of the Ottoman Empire. Gandhi is best known for helping to free the people of India from British rule through nonviolent resistance. He thus became one of the most respected spiritual and political leaders of the twentieth century. India honors him as "Father of the Nation" and as a Mahatma, or Great Soul.

Gandhi left India in 1888 to study law in London and returned to India in 1891 to practice. In 1893 he took on a one year contract to do legal work in South Africa. At the time, South Africa was controlled by the British. When he attempted to exercise his rights as a British subject he was abused, and soon realized that all ethnic Indians suffered similar treatment. Gandhi stayed in South Africa for 21 years working to improve the rights and conditions of ethnic Indians. He developed a nonviolent method of direct social action based on spiritual principles, which he called *Satyagraha*, also known as passive resistance. In 1915 Gandhi returned to India and within 15 years became the leader of the Indian nationalist movement. Using the tenets of *Satyagraha* he lead the campaign for Indian independence from Britain. Gandhi was arrested many times by the British for his activities in South Africa and India. He believed that it was honorable to suffer or go to jail for a just cause. He spent a total of seven years in prison for his political activities. More than once Gandhi used fasting to impress upon others the need to be nonviolent.

Through the efforts of Gandhi and others, India was granted independence in 1947, but partitioned in two—thus were born India and Pakistan. Rioting between Hindus and Muslims followed. Being an advocate for a united India where Hindus and Muslims could live together in peace, Gandhi began a fast at the age of 78 in order to stop the bloodshed. After five days, the opposing leaders pledged to stop the fighting and Gandhi broke his fast. Sadly, twelve days later Gandhi was assassinated by a Hindu fanatic who opposed his program of tolerance for all creeds and religions. He died with the mention of God on his lips.

Albert Einstein, the famous physicist, eulogized Gandhi saying, "Generations to come will scarcely believe that such a one as this walked the earth in flesh and blood."

Gandhian ideals

As humankind struggles to find ways of living responsibly in the "global village," many of Gandhi's teachings appear pertinent again and are receiving renewed attention. The direction of his thought is challenging and points to a holistic worldview.

Truth and nonviolence, both of which are discussed in other chapters of this book, were Gandhi's most cherished principles. Gandhi writes: "Truth resides in every human heart, and one has to search for it there, and to be guided by truth as one sees it. But no one has a right to coerce others to act according to his own view of truth."[3] Gandhi teaches that Truth is God, and that

it is our sacred duty to seek it.* If Truth was to Gandhi the Ultimate End (i.e. God), then *ahimsa* (nonviolence) was the perfect
means of attaining that end.† Gandhi writes: "Non-violence is the
greatest force man has been endowed with. Truth is the only goal
he has. For God is none other than Truth. But Truth cannot
be, never will be, reached except through non-violence... That
which distinguishes man from all other animals is his capacity to
be non-violent. And he fulfils his mission only to the extent that
he is non-violent and no more."[16] From these two fundamental
principles can be "derived" all of his other teachings:

• **Oneness and Equality of Religions**

Gandhi teaches that all faiths spring from the same ultimate, timeless, eternal Religion. He writes: "The root of all religions is one
and it is pure and all of them have sprung from the same source,
hence all are equal."[17] "Let no one even for a moment entertain
the fear that a reverent study of other religions is likely to weaken
or shake one's faith in one's own."[18] "This study of other religions
besides one's own will give one a grasp of the rock-bottom unity of
all religions and afford a glimpse also of that universal and absolute
truth which lies beyond the 'dust of creeds and faiths'."[18]

• **Sarvodaya and Collective Trusteeship**

Sarvodaya is the name given to Gandhi's ideal of nonviolent so-
cialism. Gandhi teaches that one should earn no more money than
is enough to support oneself and one's family, and advocates voluntary sharing of excess wealth. While wealth should be used
for the common good of all rather than for the private gain of a
few, Gandhi condemns its forceful redistribution: "Wealthy people should act as trustees of the wealth. But if they are robbed
of this wealth through violent means, it would not be in the interest of the country. This is known as communism. Moreover, by
adopting violent means, we would be depriving society of capable
individuals."[19]

---

*See also Chapter 2.
†See also Chapter 5

- **Village Autonomy**

Gandhi advocates independence for the common people, not just for those who rule over them. Thus, while Gandhi is best known as a freedom fighter who brought India independence from Britain, his primary aim was independence for the grassroots of society. He writes: "Independence must begin at the bottom."[20] "My idea of village *swaraj* [self-rule] is that it is a complete republic, independent of its neighbors for its own vital wants, and yet interdependent for many others in which dependence is a necessity."[21]

- **Decentralization of Power**

According to Gandhi, centralized government is inherently prone to violence. Therefore Gandhi advocates decentralization of political power. Explaining his metaphorical vision of the structure of a future nonviolent society, Gandhi writes: "Life will not be a pyramid with the apex sustained by the bottom. But it will be an oceanic circle whose centre will be the individual always ready to perish for the village, the latter ready to perish for the circle of villages, till at last the whole becomes one life composed of individuals, never aggressive in their arrogance, but ever humble, sharing the majesty of the oceanic circle of which they are integral units."[22]

- **Self-reliance**

Swadeshi (Self-reliance) is mainly understood to mean a protectionist technique that Gandhi employed against the mercantilistic policies of the British, whereby the masses were urged to abstain from cloth manufactured outside India, and instead to use cotton, silk, or wool cloth made in India. But Gandhi gives it a broader meaning: "*Swadeshi* carries a great and profound meaning. It does not mean merely the use of what is produced in one's own country. That meaning is certainly there in *swadeshi*. But there is another meaning implied in it which is far greater and much more important. *Swadeshi* means reliance on our own strength. We should also know what we mean by 'reliance on our own strength'. 'Our strength' means the strength of our body, our mind, and our soul. From among these, on which should we depend? The answer is

brief. The soul is supreme and therefore soul-force is the foundation on which man must build."[23]

• Machines

Gandhi strongly disapproved of machinery, since in his time machines typically led to the concentration of economic and political
power in the hands of a few, extremely rich people.[24] Today, of
course, the reverse appears to be possible. For example, information technology has led to decentralization, rather than centralization, of power. It would be interesting to know what Gandhi
would have to say about the Internet, for he wrote: "Every machine that helps every individual has a place. But I must confess
that I have never sat down to think out what that machine can
be."[25] "I would prize every invention of science made for the benefit of all."[26] Although Gandhi's original fears about machines have
proven unfounded, nevertheless industrialization and automation
have not automatically led to an equitable distribution of work and
leisure time.*

• Yajña and Service

Gandhi teaches that work should be done with pure motives, without desire for any type of reward, in a spirit of service. When work
is thus performed, it becomes an act of *yajña* (sacrifice). He writes:
"'*Yajña*' means an act directed to the welfare of others, done without desiring any return for it, whether of a temporal or spiritual
nature. 'Act' here must be taken in its widest sense, and includes
thoughts and word, as well as deed. 'Others' embraces not only
humanity, but all life."[27]

• Passive Resistance

The word *Satyagraha* was coined during Gandhi's lifetime to describe passive resistance, as developed and practiced by Gandhi in
South Africa. The term can be literally translated in English as
"insistence on truth." *Satyagraha* was Gandhi's nonviolent method
of resisting injustice and violence in their various manifestations.

---

*See also Chapter 10.

Essentially, it consists in nonviolent noncooperation with the protagonists of violence. As a method of last resort, Gandhi did use civil disobedience—passive resistance in its most disruptive (and violent) form. Gandhi's method of nonviolent noncooperation is a true and tried technique that has been successfully used to fight violent and systematic human rights violations in a number of states. Examples of leaders who have adapted the method include Nelson Mandela, Martin Luther King Jr., and His Holiness the Dalai Lama.

• **Human Rights and World Citizenship**

Gandhi teaches that every human right is fundamentally related to some reciprocal responsibility towards the world. He writes: "All rights to be deserved and preserved come from duty well done. Thus the very right to live accrues to us only when we do the duty of citizenship of the world. From this very fundamental statement perhaps it is easy enough to define the duties of man and woman and correlate every right to some corresponding duty to be first performed. Every other right can be shown to be a usurpation hardly worth fighting for."[28]

• **Ramarajya and World Federation**

According to Gandhi, it is possible to establish *Ramarajya*, or the Kingdom of God, on earth. Indeed, he seems to have believed in its inevitability. But before this can happen, nations must renounce violence towards each other and learn to live in peace. He explains that "a world federation is possible of realization and in that case it would not be necessary for countries to maintain armed forces."[29] "There can be no world federation of countries ruled by armies."[29]

1.3 Gandhi's Contacts with Bahá'ís

There is no doubt that Gandhi was acquainted with the Bahá'í Faith. Gandhi had personal contact with Bahá'ís.[30] Mr. Mani H. M. Mehta, then Chairman (President) of the Spiritual Assembly of the Bahá'ís of Bombay, met Gandhi and was able to share the Bahá'í teachings with him. (Incidentally, Gandhi asked Mr. Mehta, formerly a Zoroastrian, why he had changed his religion.*) On other occasions, Mrs. Shirin Fozdar, a well known Bahá'í, also met Gandhi a number of times. Some American Bahá'ís visiting India were also able to meet Gandhi during his imprisonment in 1942 at Aga Khan Palace, which had been converted into a jail.

It is also known that Martha Root, whom Shoghi Effendi called the "star-servant" of the Bahá'í Faith, mailed Gandhi a copy of *Gleanings from the Writings of Bahá'u'lláh* when she was in Surat, Gujarat, probably around 1937–38. She had visited India three times.[30] (More research will be required to trace the letter.)

Most memorable of all, of course, is Gandhi's famous phrase, "The Bahá'í Faith is a solace to humankind." These words appeared in the *Bombay Chronicle* newspaper on May 24, 1944, during the centenary of the Bahá'í Faith. (Recall that the Báb declared his mission on the evening before May 23, 1844.) The then Mayor of Bombay, Nagin Das Master, mentioned Gandhi's praise of the Bahá'í Faith in the course of his inaugural address at an event organized by the Bahá'í community of Bombay, and the *Bombay Chronicle* carried parts of his speech.[30]

---

*Religious conversion is further discussed in Section 13.3.

Chapter Notes

1. J. E. Esslemont, *Bahá'u'lláh and the New Era*, 5th rev. ed. (Wilmette: Bahá'í Publishing Trust, 1987).

2. *The Moral and Political Writings of Mahatma Gandhi*. Ed. Raghavan Iyer (Oxford: Oxford University Press, 1986).

3. *The Essential Writings of Mahatma Gandhi*. Ed. Raghavan Iyer (Oxford: Oxford University Press, 1990).

4. Eknath Easwaran, *Gandhi the Man* (Petaluma: Nilgiri Press, 1983).

5. *Bahá'u'lláh*, A statement prepared by the Bahá'í International Community's Office of Public Information New York.

6. *The Hidden Words of Bahá'u'lláh*. Trans. Shoghi Effendi (Wilmette: Bahá'í Publishing Trust, 1985), 3–4.

7. *Paris Talks: Addresses given by 'Abdu'l-Bahá in Paris in 1911–1912* (London: Bahá'í Publishing Trust, 1972), 143.

8. *Gleanings from the Writings of Bahá'u'lláh*. Trans. Shoghi Effendi (Wilmette: Bahá'í Publishing Trust, 1976), 287–288.

9. 'Abdu'l-Bahá, quoted in J. E. Esslemont, *Bahá'u'lláh and the New Era*, 5th rev. ed. (Wilmette: Bahá'í Publishing Trust, 1987), 147.

10. 'Abdu'l-Bahá, quoted in J. E. Esslemont, *Bahá'u'lláh and the New Era*, 5th rev. ed. (Wilmette: Bahá'í Publishing Trust, 1987), 149.

11. *Gleanings from the Writings of Bahá'u'lláh*, 259–260.

12. *The Hidden Words of Bahá'u'lláh*. Trans. Shoghi Effendi (Wilmette: Bahá'í Publishing Trust, 1985), 41.

13. *Gleanings from the Writings of Bahá'u'lláh*, 95.

14. 'Abdu'l-Bahá, quoted in *Bahá'u'lláh and the New Era*, 160–161.

15. Shoghi Effendi, quoted in *Bahá'u'lláh and the New Era*, 281–282.

16. *The Essential Writings of Mahatma Gandhi*, 240–1.

17. *The Essential Writings of Mahatma Gandhi*, 160.

18. *The Essential Writings of Mahatma Gandhi*, 150.

19. *The Essential Writings of Mahatma Gandhi*, 408.

20. *The Essential Writings of Mahatma Gandhi*, 347.

21. *The Essential Writings of Mahatma Gandhi*, 358.

22. *The Essential Writings of Mahatma Gandhi*, 348.

23. *The Essential Writings of Mahatma Gandhi*, 362.
24. See, for example, *The Essential Writings of Mahatma Gandhi*. Ed. Raghavan Iyer (Oxford: Oxford University Press, 1990), 348.
25. *The Essential Writings of Mahatma Gandhi*, 348–9.
26. *The Essential Writings of Mahatma Gandhi*, 402.
27. *The Essential Writings of Mahatma Gandhi*, 379.
28. *The Essential Writings of Mahatma Gandhi*, 392–3.
29. *The Essential Writings of Mahatma Gandhi*, 409.
30. The information regarding Gandhi's contacts with Bahá'ís has been kindly provided by the National Spiritual Assembly of the Bahá'ís of India (Personal communication from Dr. A. K. Merchant, Office of External Affairs, National Spiritual Assembly of the Bahá'ís of India, 7 October 1998).

Chapter 2

The Quest for Truth

Chernobyl's number 4 nuclear reactor was completely destroyed on 26 April 1986 by explosions that blew the roof off the reactor building and released large amounts of radioactive material into the environment. It was the most serious nuclear accident in history. The nuclear "cloud" included the dangerous radioactive isotopes of iodine and cesium, that can be deadly to humans and the environment. The iodine isotopes delivered harmful radiation to children who had inhaled it or ingested it via contaminated milk. At first, the world outside the Soviet Union knew more about what was happening than the resident victims. On April 28 a Swedish monitoring station noticed rising levels of radioactivity. Further analysis revealed a very strange brew of extremely rare isotopes, a combination normally produced only by an atomic explosion or a major nuclear reactor meltdown. One of the isotopes found was ruthenium, which melts at an extremely high temperature of more than 2250 degrees centigrade—a temperature normally found only in places such as the sun, a melting nuclear reactor, or a nuclear bomb! Sweden announced the findings and made diplomatic inquiries to Moscow, but at first the latter admitted to nothing. Only later did Moscow concede the occurrence of a small and insignificant accident—a quick and minor release of radioactivity. Is such behavior—reminiscent of many bungled "cover-ups" in other countries—consistent with commitment to truth, freedom of expression and freedom to investigate independently? No. Indeed, until the Chernobyl disaster, the Soviet Union had been secretive. Few journalists were allowed in the country except under controlled circumstances and the Soviet media, controlled by the government, usually did not admit to any weakness or error. The Soviet press was used to extol the superiority of Soviet progress and technology. Truth had become less important than ideology. One may be tempted to wonder whether such degenerate values indirectly precipitated the impending collapse of the Soviet Union. When commitment to truth fades, false ideas and theories—bankrupt and pernicious—can begin to take root in individuals and institutions. Frustration and failure inevitably follow when truth is neglected or not properly valued. There is little doubt that commitment to truth must become a core principle animating efforts towards a nonviolent civilization. Hence, it is instructive to take a closer look at the nature of truth.

Abstract reasoning and self-reflective intelligence distinguish the human mind from those of our animal cousins. Humans have an instinctual urge to seek out truth. Indeed, so strong is our drive to learn new things and grow in understanding that we sometimes willingly submit to suffering in order to transcend our limits. A seemingly unquenchable thirst for discovery, adventure, intellectual curiosity, experimentation, and philosophical enquiry is a fundamental characteristic of the searching mind. Search is a prerequisite to discovery.

To find truth, we need to have some idea of what it is we really seek. What exactly is truth? There are a number of ways to think about this matter. In traditional logic, true and false propositions are considered to be opposites. Neither is considered more fundamental than the other. A different approach is suggested by the *Upanishads*:[1] truth is that which cannot be shown to be false. A related conception of truth may be inferred from Plato's metaphor of the cave in *The Republic*, his classical philosophical work on the nature of justice: truth relates to the hidden, "ideal" order that underlies and sustains the world in which we live.[2] Truth pertains to the timeless, ideal Reality that generates everything in our world. This human world is merely a "shadow" of the true reality. We can turn to the philosophy of science for other perspectives. Many physicists, for example, identify the quest for truth with the search for the universal laws of Nature that govern the processes that generate and sustain everything known in the universe. In a related atheist view, a "God" did not directly create the universe, but rather the laws of Nature are the true generating principles that "created" the universe. There are many other interesting ways of thinking about truth.[2]

How best to seek truth, assuming one already knows its definition? Again, there are a number of approaches to this question. The scientific method represents one attempted answer. In this view, experiment and observation are the touchstones that distinguish truth from error. Scientists often "test" a hypothesis by comparing its predictions with those of a "null hypothesis." Science works because it introduces "objective" criteria for ascertaining what is true and what is not. Hence, two or more hypotheses can be tested against experimental data. This reliance of science on objectivity makes it extremely difficult to apply the scientific method to phenomena that are intrinsically subjective in nature, such as highly personal, mystical, or spiritual experiences. This is one major cause of the traditional reluctance of science to venture into matters of religion and spirituality. Science is only now starting seriously and systematically to study subjective phenomena.

Notwithstanding, from time immemorial it has been possible to apply a rational approach to seeking truth in our daily lives. Every human being can "test" the truth of an idea against "evidence" drawn from personal experience. (In this light, it is interesting to note that Gandhi named his autobiography *My Experiments with Truth*.) It may be true that a single person cannot be as objective as a community of many highly trained individuals, but if it were not possible for individuals to seek out truth with some degree of objectivity, then it would also not be possible to think independently! Indeed, it is very much within an individual's power to attempt to think without bias and prejudice. The will to undertake dispassionate analysis—with humility, free from bias, and without emotional attachment—is a key to success in recognizing truth when we stumble upon it.

The teachings of Gandhi and of the Bahá'í Faith both stress the need to be committed to the pursuit of truth. This chapter examines what they each say about truth and how to seek it.

2.1   Independent Investigation

Gandhi taught that truth must be sought independently. Explaining how each person must be guided by their own independent understanding of truth, Gandhi writes,

> Truth resides in every human heart, and one has to search for it there, and to be guided by truth as one sees it. But no one has a right to coerce others to act according to his own view of truth.[3]

Bahá'ís hold similar views. Central to the Bahá'í Faith is the teaching that each individual must seek out truth independently. Poetically personifying truth in the first person, Bahá'u'lláh writes in the *Hidden Words*,

> O Son of Spirit! The best beloved of all things in My sight is Justice; turn not away therefrom if thou desirest Me, and neglect it not that I may confide in thee. By its aid thou shalt see with thine own eyes and not through the eyes of others, and shalt know of thine own knowledge and not through the knowledge of thy neighbor. Ponder this in thy heart; how it behooveth thee to be. Verily justice is My gift to thee and the sign of My loving-kindness. Set it then before thine eyes.[4]

2.2   Absolute Truth

All human beings are capable of grasping truths to varying degrees. These truths can be considered relative, in the sense that their veracity is dependent on the validity of underlying assumptions or theories.[5] They are relative also in the sense that no finite human mind can grasp truth in all its entirety. Nevertheless, our very ability to imagine the possibility of knowing truth in its totality leads naturally to the concept of absolute Truth.

Gandhi identified absolute Truth with God, and therefore he considered the existence of God to be almost tautological:

> There was a time when I doubted the existence of God, but even at that time I did not doubt the existence of

> truth. This Truth is not a material quality... It is
> God because it rules the whole universe.[6]

He also believed that the identification of Truth with God is the
clearest definition of God, and that this definition can provide an
opportunity for theists and atheists to find common ground in
terminology:

> I found that the nearest approach to Truth is through
> love. But I found also that love has many meanings...
> It is very difficult to understand 'God is love' because of
> a variety of meanings of love, but I never found a dou-
> ble meaning in connection with Truth and not even the
> atheists have denied the necessity or power of Truth.
> Not only so. In their passion for discovering Truth,
> they have not hesitated even to deny the very existence
> of God—from their own point of view rightly. And it
> was because of their reasoning that I saw that I was not
> going to say 'God is Truth,' but 'Truth is God.' There-
> fore I recall the name of Charles Bradlaugh—a great
> Englishman who lived 50 years ago.* He delighted to
> call himself an atheist. But knowing as I do some-
> thing of his life, I never considered him an atheist. I
> would call him a god-fearing man although he would
> reject that claim, and I know his face would redden. I
> would say: No, Mr. Bradlaugh, you are a truth-fearing
> man, not a god-fearing man, and I would disarm his
> criticisms by saying 'Truth is God' as I have disarmed
> criticisms of many a young man.[7]

The idea that absolute Truth is God can also be found in the
earliest Bahá'í sacred texts.[8] The Báb said that the "Lord, the
One true God, is none other than the Sovereign Truth."[9] Later
texts also contain such references. In the Kitáb-i-Aqdas (the Most
Holy Book of the Bahá'í Faith) Bahá'u'lláh refers to God as the
"Sovereign Truth," "the Eternal Truth," and also simply as "the
Truth."[10] 'Abdu'l-Bahá also refers to God as "the Truth."[11] Explaining how finite minds can never grasp the whole Truth (God),
but only partial truths, 'Abdu'l-Bahá writes,

---

*1833–1891, British social reformer and member of Parliament, a secularist.

The pictures of Divinity that come to our mind are the
product of our fancy; they exist in the realm of our
imagination. They are not adequate to the Truth...
therefore, the Divinity which man can understand is
partial; it is not complete. ˙ Divinity is actual Truth
and real existence, and not any representation of it.
Divinity itself contains All, and is not contained.[12]

Moreover, the Bahá'í writings frequently refer to divinity as th
"Sun of Truth."[13] 'Abdu'l-Bahá writes,

Truth may be likened to the sun! The sun is the luminous body that disperses all shadows; in the same way
does truth scatter the shadows of our imagination. As
the sun gives life to the body of humanity so does truth
give life to their souls. Truth is a sun that rises from
different points on the horizon.[14]

The sun is the life-giver to the physical bodies of all
creatures upon earth; without its warmth their growth
would be stunted, their development would be arrested,
they would decay and die. Even so do the souls of men
need the Sun of Truth to shed its rays upon their souls,
to develop them, to educate and encourage them. As
the sun is to the body of a man so is the Sun of Truth
to his soul.[15]

It is interesting that in *The Gita According to Gandhi,* we find
the same Sun of Truth mentioned in the book's introduction, by
Mahadev Desai:

The Truth has been revealed over and over again and
will go on being revealed until the end of time. We
hear it said that there is nothing new under the sun.
Well, there need be nothing new, for the Sun of Truth,
exhaustless in his manifestations, ever presents aspects
and visions new.[16]

In view of such statements, the rest of this chapter uses the
words Truth and God almost interchangeably.

2.3 Search and Spirituality

Why search for truth? Many scientists search for scientific truth, and it is not uncommon for people to be motivated by a desire to seek truth for truth's sake alone. Indeed, this is a noble ideal. However, to Gandhi and to many Bahá'ís, the quest for truth is more than an end in itself. The belief held by Gandhi and the Bahá'ís, that Truth is divine, adds a mystical or spiritual dimension to the quest for truth.

Explaining why we must search for truth, Gandhi writes,

> If we had attained the full vision of Truth, we would no longer be mere seekers, but would have become one with God, for Truth is God. But being only seekers, we prosecute our quest, and are conscious of our imperfection.[17]

> No search is possible without some workable assumptions. If we grant nothing, we find nothing. Ever since its commencement, the world, the wise and the foolish included, has proceeded upon the assumption that if we are, God is, and that if God is not, we are not... The very search for Truth becomes interesting and worthwhile, because of this belief. But search for Truth is search for God. Truth is God. God is, because Truth is. We embark upon the search, because we believe that there is Truth and that it can be found by diligent search and meticulous observance of the well-known and well-tried rules of search. There is no record in history of the failure of such search. Even the atheists who have pretended to disbelieve in God have believed in Truth. The trick they have performed is that of giving God another, not a new, name. His names are legion. Truth is the crown of them all.[18]

Gandhi also felt that devotion to Truth and a commitment to seeking it are prerequisites to further personal development:

> Devotion to Truth is the sole justification for our existence. All our activities should be centered in truth.

Truth should be the very breath of our life. When once
this stage in the pilgrim's progress is reached, all other
rules of correct living will come without effort and obedience to them will be instinctive. But without Truth
it is impossible to observe any principles or rules in
life.[19]

The idea that the search for truth is a tool for spiritual enlight-
enment can also be found in the Bahá'í writings:

O thou seeker of the True One! If thou wishest the divine knowledge and recognition, purify thy heart from
all beside God, be wholly attracted to the ideal, beloved
One; search for and choose Him and apply thyself to
rational and authoritative arguments. For arguments
are a guide to the path and by this the heart will be
turned unto the Sun of Truth. And when the heart is
turned unto the Sun, then the eye will be opened and
will recognize the Sun through the Sun itself.[20]

Bahá'ís believe it is an individual's sacred duty to seek out truth.
The quest for truth moreover acquires a romantic or mystical qual-
ity when people regard the search for Truth to be identical with
the search for God.[21] Bahá'u'lláh gives a glimpse of the burning
passion which can accompany such search:

The true seeker hunteth naught but the object of his
quest, and the lover hath no desire save union with his
beloved. Nor shall the seeker reach his goal unless he
sacrifice all things. That is, whatever he hath seen, and
heard, and understood, all must he set at naught, that
he may enter the realm of the spirit, which is the City
of God. Labor is needed, if we are to seek Him; ardor is
needed, if we are to drink of the honey of reunion with
Him; and if we taste of this cup, we shall cast away the
world. On this journey the traveler abideth in every
land and dwelleth in every region. In every face, he
seeketh the beauty of the Friend; in every country he
looketh for the Beloved. He joineth every company,
and seeketh fellowship with every soul, that haply in

some mind he may uncover the secret of the Friend, or in some face he may behold the beauty of the Loved One.[22]

2.4 The Danger of Blind Imitation

A belief shared by Gandhi and the Bahá'ís is that blind imitation of religious and cultural traditions can be harmful. Forced slavery, for example, used to be a tradition in some cultures, but the continuation of this practice today would amount to an unconscionable injustice and crime, deserving severe punishment.

All traditions which cease to be beneficial should be discarded in the best interests of humanity. Warning about blind imitation, 'Abdu'l-Bahá writes,

> First, man must independently investigate reality, for the disagreements and dissensions which afflict and affect humanity primarily proceed from imitations of ancestral beliefs and adherences to hereditary forms of worship. These imitations are accidental and without sanction in the Holy Books. They are the outcomes of human interpretations and teachings which have arisen, gradually obscuring the real light of divine meaning and causing men to differ and dissent. The reality proclaimed in the heavenly Books and divine teachings is ever conducive to love, unity and fellowship.[23]

Gandhi held almost identical views on this subject:

> I do not hold that everything ancient is good because it is ancient. I do not advocate surrender of [the] God-given reasoning faculty in the face of ancient tradition. Any tradition, however ancient, if inconsistent with morality, is fit to be banished from the land. Untouchability* may be considered to be an ancient tradition, and even so many an ancient horrible belief and super-

---

*People who were considered ritually unclean and who typically cleaned the human waste in "latrines."

stitious practice. I would sweep them out of existence
if I had the power.[24]

2.5   The True Seeker

While on the one hand it may be relatively easy to grasp the concept of truth, on the other hand it can be rather challenging to
remain dedicated to it at all times. It may interest the reader to
compare what Gandhi and the Bahá'í Faith have to say about the
quest for truth.

Commenting on the prerequisites for successfully seeking truth,
based on his own experiences, Gandhi writes,

> Truth is that which you believe to be true at this mo-
> ment, and that is your God. If a man worships this
> relative truth, he is sure to attain the Absolute Truth,
> i.e., God, in the course of time.[25]

> I am devoted to none but Truth and I owe no discipline
> to anybody but Truth.[25]

> I am but a humble seeker after Truth and bent upon
> finding it. I count no sacrifice too great for the sake
> of seeing God face to face. The whole of my activity
> whether it may be called social, political, humanitar-
> ian or ethical is directed to that end. And as I know
> that God is found more often in the lowliest of His
> creatures than in the high and mighty, I am struggling
> to reach the status of these. I cannot do so without
> their service. Hence my passion for the service of the
> suppressed classes.[26]

> The instruments for the quest of Truth are as simple as
> they are difficult. They may appear quite impossible to
> an arrogant person, and quite possible to an innocent
> child. The seeker after truth should be humbler than
> the dust.[17]

> ... it is impossible for us to realize perfect Truth so long
> as we are imprisoned in this mortal frame. We can only

visualize it in our imagination. We cannot, through the instrumentality of this ephemeral body, see face to face Truth which is eternal. That is why in the last resort one must depend on faith.[26]

It is faith that steers us through stormy seas, faith that moves mountains and faith that jumps across the ocean. That faith is nothing but a living, wide-awake consciousness of God within. He who has achieved that faith wants nothing. Bodily diseased, he is spiritually healthy; physically poor, he rolls in spiritual riches.[27]

God can never be realized by one who is not pure of heart. Self-purification therefore must mean purification in all walks of life. And purification being highly infectious, purification of oneself necessarily leads to the purification of one's surroundings.[28]

But the path of self-purification is hard and steep. To attain to perfect purity one has to become absolutely passion-free in thought, speech, and action; to rise above the opposing currents of love and hatred, attachment and repulsion.[28]

If you would swim on the bosom of the ocean of Truth, you must reduce yourself to a zero.[3]

Some of these themes are reminiscent of those found in the teachings of the Bahá'í Faith. In one of the celebrated passages of the Kitáb-i-Íqán (Book of Certitude), Bahá'u'lláh describes the attributes of the true seeker:

... O my brother, when a true seeker determineth to take the step of search in the path leading to the knowledge of the Ancient of Days, he must, before all else, cleanse and purify his heart, which is the seat of the revelation of the inner mysteries of God, from the obscuring dust of all acquired knowledge, and the allusions of the embodiments of satanic fancy. He must purge his breast, which is the sanctuary of the abiding love of the Beloved, of every defilement, and sanctify his soul from all that pertaineth to water and clay, from all shadowy and ephemeral attachments. He must so cleanse his heart that no remnant of either love or hate may linger therein, lest that love blindly incline him to error, or that hate repel him away from the truth. Even as thou dost witness in this day how most of the people, because of such love and hate, are bereft of the immortal Face, have strayed far from the Embodiments of the divine mysteries, and, shepherdless, are roaming through the wilderness of oblivion and error. That seeker must at all times put his trust in God, must renounce the peoples of the earth, detach himself from the world of dust, and cleave unto Him Who is the Lord of Lords. He must never seek to exalt himself above any one, must wash away from the tablet of his heart every trace of pride and vainglory, must cling unto patience and resignation, observe silence, and refrain from idle talk. For the tongue is a smouldering fire, and excess of speech a deadly poison. Material fire consumeth the body, whereas the fire of the tongue devoureth both heart and soul. The force of the former lasteth but for a time, whilst the effects of the latter endure a century.

That seeker should also regard backbiting as grievous error, and keep himself aloof from its dominion, inasmuch as backbiting quencheth the light of the heart, and extinguisheth the life of the soul. He should be content with little, and be freed from all inordinate desire. He should treasure the companionship of those that have renounced the world, and regard avoidance of boastful and worldly people a precious benefit. At the dawn of every day he should commune with God, and with all his soul persevere in the quest of his Beloved. He should consume every wayward thought with the flame of His loving mention, and, with the swiftness of lightning, pass by all else save Him. He should succour the dispossessed, and never withhold his favour from the destitute. He should show kindness to animals, how much more unto his fellow-man, to him who is endowed with the power of utterance. He should not hesitate to offer up his life for his Beloved, nor allow the censure of the people to turn him away from the Truth. He should not wish for others that which he doth not wish for himself, nor promise that which he doth not fulfil. With all his heart should the seeker avoid fellowship with evil doers, and pray for the remission of their sins. He should forgive the sinful, and never despise his low estate, for none knoweth what his own end shall be. How often hath a sinner, at the hour of death, attained to the essence of faith, and, quaffing the immortal draught, hath taken his flight unto the celestial Concourse. And how often hath a devout believer, at the hour of his soul's ascension, been so changed as to fall into the nethermost fire. Our purpose in revealing these convincing and weighty utterances is to impress upon the seeker that he should regard all else beside God as transient, and count all things save Him, Who is the Object of all adoration, as utter nothingness.[29]

Chapter Notes

1. The *Upanishads* contain the highest form of philosophical introspection in Hinduism and and are seen as perennial sources of spiritual knowledge. There are ten principal *Upanishads*.

2. For a more rigorous philosophical discussion about truth, consult philosophy textbooks, e.g., M. Velasquez, *Philosophy: A Text with Readings*, 6th ed. (Belmont: Wadsworth Publishing Company, 1997).

3. *All Men Are Brothers: Life and Thoughts of Mahatma Gandhi as Told in His Own Words*. Ed. K Kripalani (Paris: UNESCO, 1969), 71.

4. *The Hidden Words of Bahá'u'lláh*. Trans. Shoghi Effendi (Wilmette: Bahá'í Publishing Trust, 1985), 3–4.

5. E.g., while it may be true that parallel lines never meet in Euclidean space, this "truth" is not necessarily true in non-Euclidean geometry.

6. *The Moral and Political Writings of Mahatma Gandhi. Volume II: Truth and Non-Violence*. Ed. Raghavan Iyer (Oxford: Oxford University Press, 1986), 172.

7. *The Moral and Political Writings of Mahatma Gandhi*, 165–6.

8. *Selections from the Writings of the Báb* (Haifa: Bahá'í World Centre, 1982). See pp. 44, 29, 18, 51.

9. *Selections from the Writings of the Báb*, 69.

10. *Kitáb-i-Aqdas* (Haifa: Bahá'í World Centre, 1992). For "Eternal Truth" see p. 39. For "Truth" see p. 208. For "Sovereign Truth" see p. 232.

11. *Tablets of 'Abdu'l-Bahá* (Chicago: Bahá'í Publishing Society, 1908). See pp. 154, 281, 288.

12. *'Abdu'l-Bahá in London: Addresses, and Notes of Conversations*. (London: Bahá'í Publishing Trust, 1982), 22.

13. In the Bahá'í writings, terms such as "Sun of Truth" refer primarily to the Manifestations of God, e.g. Jesus, Krishna, etc. See Chapter 3 for details.

14. *Paris Talks: Addresses given by 'Abdu'l-Bahá in Paris in 1911–1912* (London: Bahá'í Publishing Trust, 1972), 128.

15. *Paris Talks,* 30.

16. *The Gospel of Selfless Action or The Gita According to Gandhi.* Ed. Mahadev Desai (Ahmedabad: Navajivan Publishing House, 1984), 65.

17. *All Men Are Brothers,* 67.

18. *All Men Are Brothers,* 65–6.

19. *The Moral and Political Writings of Mahatma Gandhi,* 162.

20. *Tablets of 'Abdu'l-Bahá,* 168.

21. Parallels between romantic and erotic desire on the one hand, and passion for truth and God on the other, can be found not only in Eastern philosophy and mysticism, but also in Western radical theology. Søren Kierkegaard, for example, gave emphasis on one's relationship to God rather than on rational objective analysis. See M. Velasquez, *Philosophy: A Text with Readings,* 6th ed. (Belmont: Wadsworth Publishing Company, 1997).

22. *The Seven Valleys and the Four Valleys* (Wilmette: Bahá'í Publishing Trust, 1991), 5.

23. *The Promulgation of Universal Peace: Talks Delivered by 'Abdu'l-Bahá during His Visit to the United States and Canada in 1912* (Wilmette: Bahá'í Publishing Trust, 1982), 314.

24. *All Men Are Brothers,* 76.

25. *All Men Are Brothers,* 72.

26. *All Men Are Brothers,* 75.

27. *All Men Are Brothers,* 69.

28. *All Men Are Brothers,* 59.

29. *Kitáb-i-Íqán* (Wilmette: Bahá'í Publishing Trust, 1989), 193–5.

Chapter 3

The Role of Religion

Religion has historically played important roles in most civilizations, hence it is worthwhile to consider it in some depth. The English word "religion" comes from a Latin word meaning to rejoin or re-unite, but sadly religion has been used as an instrument of division—even of war. God and religion have been controversial topics for the last few centuries, partly because religion has often been used as a tool of oppression. In the middle ages, for example, Christians waged the Crusades against Muslims for almost two centuries. More recently, Protestants and Catholics killed one another in parts of Europe, such as Ireland, notwithstanding each sect's claim to follow the same Jesus Christ, whose teaching was to "love thy neighbor as thyself." Sectarian violence has also plagued the followers of Islam, Hinduism and other religions. In Gandhi's native land, Hindus and Muslims have a long history of bloodshed. Even when religion has not led directly to war, it has sometimes been manipulated to perpetrate systematic human rights abuses. Examples of religious oppression include the Inquisition in Europe, and more recently, the massacre and subsequent persecution of the Bahá'ís in Iran. In yet other cases, the role of religion in oppression has been more subtle, for instance the treatment of Hindu "untouchables," especially before Indian independence. Other examples include the fate of Jews, Gypsies and other European minorities during the Nazi years. Religion's ugly role as a tool of oppression has led to much apathy, even prompting some people to conclude that religion is intrinsically bad. Religion is the opiate of the masses, declared Karl Marx. We can wonder whether he realized that communism would lead to similar—if not worse—tyranny. Ironically, it has even been argued that communism is a religion—an atheistic religion! For these and many other reasons, religion has become a confusing matter for many people. Indeed, it has even been questioned whether the spirit of religion that characterized the golden ages of the world's great faiths has survived, or whether it has gone extinct. Neitzsche, after all, wrote that "God is dead." Such diverging views about God and religion have tended to become isolated from one another, further frustrating the emergence of consensus. The root cause of all this apathy and confusion, it can be argued, is the following: religion has been used to divide and oppress rather than to liberate and unite the peoples of the world.

Such abuse of religion stems in large part due to the way in which it is practiced—or not practiced, as the case may be. Very often in the past, religion has been followed rather blindly. For example, sons and daughters often follow the religion of their parents without even learning about the rudiments of their own faith—let alone other faiths! The son of a Hindu becomes a Hindu, the daughter of a Christian becomes a Christian. Instances of independent investigation in religion are indeed exceptions to the general rule. Likewise, the followers of religions have been all too happy to follow the dictates of their priests—again, blindly. Such blind faith, combined with self-righteous religious zealotry, is a deadly, volatile mixture. How many the Hindus and Muslims who perished in Gandhi's native land because of religious incitement by their avowed leaders? How many the Bahá'ís who were violently martyred at the hands of blind followers of the Muslim clergy? Gandhi and the Bahá'ís believe that this state of affairs is seriously wrong. As discussed in the previous chapter, truth must be sought out independently by each individual. If done correctly, an unbiased study of religion cannot but reveal to the seeker the many elements that the world faiths have in common.

Gandhi and the Bahá'ís both uphold the Oneness of God and the essential oneness of religion. Specifically, both accept the divine origin and purpose of all of the major world religions, including the Hindu, Jewish, Zoroastrian, Buddhist, Christian, and Muslim faiths among others, as discussed below.* This chapter further explores the concept of God and religion, as found in the writings of Gandhi and of the Bahá'í Faith. God is Truth, or rather, "Truth is God," according to Gandhi. Hence, the question of the existence of God does not even arise, because belief in Truth is tautological. This point of view is also consistent with Bahá'í beliefs.† Bahá'u'lláh explains that God can be compared to the "Sun of Truth." This Sun cannot be directly perceived by humankind, hence the need for Prophets and *Avatars*.‡ These "Manifestations of God," such as Krishna, Jesus, and Muhammad, are successive "Mirrors" that reflect the Light of the Sun of Truth. Their Light is none other than the "Holy Spirit" of God. This explanation contains the essence of the Bahá'í teachings about God and religion. It is also, to a large extent, consistent with Gandhi's views.

3.1 God Beyond Description

God, Bahá'u'lláh says, is "sanctified above all attributes and holy above all names."[1] Gandhi's beliefs about the transcendent nature of God are practically identical to those of the Bahá'ís:

> The Supreme can be described neither as Being nor as non-Being. It is beyond definition or description, above all attributes.[2]

Gandhi specifically rejected anthropomorphic ideas about God:

> God is not a person... God is the force. He is the essence of life. He is pure and undefiled consciousness. He is eternal. And yet, strangely enough, all are not able to derive either benefit from or shelter in the all-pervading living presence. Electricity is a powerful force. Not all can benefit from it. It can only be produced by following certain laws. It is a lifeless force. Man can utilize it if he labours hard enough to acquire

---

*See also Chapter 1.
†See also Chapter 2.
‡The concept of *Avatar* is discussed in Section 3.2.

the knowledge of its laws. The living force which we call God can similarly be found if we know and follow His law leading to the discovery of Him in us.[3]

However, this impersonal aspect of God does not keep Gandhi from experiencing the immanence of God in everything:

> To me God is Truth and Love; God is ethics and morality; God is fearlessness. God is the source of Light and Life and yet He is above and beyond all these. God is conscience. He is even the atheism of the atheist... He transcends speech and reason... He is a personal God to those who need His personal presence. He is embodied to those who need His touch. He is the purest essence. He simply *is* to those who have faith. He is all things to all men. He is in us and yet above and beyond us... He is long-suffering. He is patient but He is also terrible... With Him ignorance is no excuse. And withal He is ever forgiving for He always gives us the chance to repent.[4]

> God is wholly good. There is no evil in Him. God made man in His own image. Unfortunately for us, man has fashioned Him in his own. This arrogation has landed mankind in a sea of troubles. God is the Supreme Alchemist. In His presence all iron and dross turn into pure gold. Similarly does all evil turn into good.[5]

Bahá'u'lláh alludes to this seemingly impossible and paradoxical "immanence-transcendence" of God in the following beautiful prayer:

> Lauded and glorified art Thou, O Lord, my God! How can I make mention of Thee, assured as I am that no tongue, however deep its wisdom, can befittingly magnify Thy name, nor can the bird of the human heart, however great its longing, ever hope to ascend into the heaven of Thy majesty and knowledge.

> If I describe Thee, O my God, as Him Who is the All-Perceiving, I find myself compelled to admit that They

Who are the highest Embodiments of perception have been created by virtue of Thy behest. And if I extol Thee as Him Who is the All-Wise, I, likewise, am forced to recognize that the Well Springs of wisdom have themselves been generated through the operation of Thy Will. And if I proclaim Thee as the Incomparable One, I soon discover that they Who are the inmost essence of oneness have been sent down by Thee and are but the evidences of Thine handiwork. And if I acclaim Thee as the Knower of all things, I must confess that they Who are the Quintessence of knowledge are but the creation and instruments of Thy Purpose.

Exalted, immeasurably exalted, art Thou above the strivings of mortal man to unravel Thy mystery, to describe Thy glory, or even to hint at the nature of Thine Essence. For whatever such strivings may accomplish, they never can hope to transcend the limitations imposed upon Thy creatures, inasmuch as these efforts are actuated by Thy decree, and are begotten of Thine invention. The loftiest sentiments which the holiest of saints can express in praise of Thee, and the deepest wisdom which the most learned of men can utter in their attempts to comprehend Thy nature, all revolve around that Center Which is wholly subjected to Thy sovereignty, Which adoreth Thy Beauty, and is propelled through the movement of Thy Pen.

Nay, forbid it, O my God, that I should have uttered such words as must of necessity imply the existence of any direct relationship between the Pen of Thy Revelation and the essence of all created things. Far, far are They Who are related to Thee above the conception of such relationship! All comparisons and likenesses fail to do justice to the Tree of Thy Revelation, and every way is barred to the comprehension of the Manifestation of Thy Self and the Day Spring of Thy Beauty.

Far, far from Thy glory be what mortal man can affirm of Thee, or attribute unto Thee, or the praise with

which he can glorify Thee! Whatever duty Thou hast
prescribed unto Thy servants of extolling to the utmost
Thy majesty and glory is but a token of Thy grace
unto them, that they may be enabled to ascend unto
the station conferred upon their own inmost being, the
station of the knowledge of their own selves.

No one else besides Thee hath, at any time, been able to
fathom Thy mystery, or befittingly to extol Thy great-
ness. Unsearchable and high above the praise of men
wilt Thou remain for ever. There is none other God
but Thee, the Inaccessible, the Omnipotent, the Om-
niscient, the Holy of Holies.[6]

3.2   The Manifestations of God

If God is "sanctified above all attributes" and "holy above all
names," Bahá'u'lláh explains, then it must be impossible to know
God's Essence directly. Hence, human beings are limited in their
ability to know and experience the attributes of God. Everything
under the sun reflects the attributes of God to varying degrees. The
greatest, most excellent, most complete manifestation of God's attributes is found in the human mind. And amongst these, the
supreme, most resplendent mind is that of the Manifestation of
God, also known as the Prophet, the Buddha, or the *Avatara*.*
Bahá'u'lláh explains further:

To every discerning and illuminated heart it is evident
that God, the unknowable Essence, the Divine Being, is
immensely exalted beyond every human attribute, such
as corporeal existence, ascent and descent, egress and
regress. Far be it from His glory that human tongue
should adequately recount His praise, or that human
heart comprehend His fathomless mystery . . .

The door of the knowledge of the Ancient of Days being
thus closed in the face of all beings, the Source of infinite grace, according to His saying, "His grace hath

---

* *Avatara* is the original Sanskrit word from which is derived the more
familiar form *Avatar*.

transcended all things; My grace hath encompassed them all," hath caused those luminous Gems of Holiness to appear out of the realm of the spirit, in the noble form of the human temple, and be made manifest unto all men, that they may impart unto the world the mysteries of the unchangeable Being, and tell of the subtleties of His imperishable Essence.

These sanctified Mirrors, these Day Springs of ancient glory, are, one and all, the Exponents on earth of Him Who is the central Orb of the universe, its Essence and ultimate Purpose. From Him proceed their knowledge and power; from Him is derived their sovereignty. The beauty of their countenance is but a reflection of His image, and their revelation a sign of His deathless glory. They are the Treasuries of Divine knowledge, and the Repositories of celestial wisdom. Through them is transmitted a grace that is infinite, and by them is revealed the Light that can never fade... These Tabernacles of Holiness, these Primal Mirrors which reflect the light of unfading glory, are but expressions of Him Who is the Invisible of the Invisibles. By the revelation of these Gems of Divine virtue all the names and attributes of God, such as knowledge and power, sovereignty and dominion, mercy and wisdom, glory, bounty, and grace, are made manifest.[7]

Examples of these Manifestations include Moses, Krishna, Buddha, Jesus Christ, and Muhammad, among many others. Bahá'ís believe that there have always been Manifestations of God in every age and that there always will be. The two most recent ones—the latest, but by no means the last—are the Báb and Bahá'u'lláh. Bahá'ís believe that Bahá'u'lláh is the Manifestation of God for this age.

Gandhi's understanding of the Hindu concept of *Avatara* is remarkably similar to the Bahá'í concept of the Manifestation of God. The word *Avatara* comes from a Sanskrit root meaning "to descend," and implies the descent of God into the world of mortals, as an "Incarnation" of God. Gandhi writes:

In Hinduism, incarnation [of God] is ascribed to one
who has performed some extraordinary service of
mankind. All embodied life is in reality an incarnation of God, but it is not usual to consider every living being as incarnation. Future generations pay this
homage to one who, in his own generation, has been
extraordinarily religious in his conduct... There is an
Urdu saying which means "Adam is not God but he is
a spark of the Divine." And therefore he who is the
most religiously behaved has most of the divine spark
in him. It is in accordance with this train of thought,
that Krishna enjoys, in Hinduism, the status of the
most perfect incarnation.[8]

It is also interesting to note that Gandhi does not interpret "incarnation" literally to mean that God is born in human "flesh."
Rather, he seems to believe, like the Bahá'ís, that the "descent"
of God into human form is a metaphor.* Commenting on the celebrated passage from the *Bhagavad Gita*[9] in which Lord Krishna
declares that he is reborn from age to age to "save the righteous,
to destroy the wicked, and to re-establish Right," Gandhi writes:

Here is comfort for the faithful and affirmation of the
truth that Right ever prevails. An eternal conflict between Right and Wrong goes on. Sometimes the latter
seems to get the upper hand, but it is Right which
ultimately prevails. The good are never destroyed,
for Right—which is Truth—cannot perish; the wicked
are destroyed, because Wrong has no independent existence. Knowing this let man cease to arrogate to
himself authorship and eschew untruth, violence and
evil. Inscrutable Providence—the unique power of the
Lord—is ever at work. This in fact is *avatara*, incarnation. Strictly speaking there can be no birth for God.[10]

The last two sentences show that Gandhi did not interpret "incarnation" anthropomorphically. It is also fascinating to note that
Gandhi states above that evil has no independent existence. Ex-

---

*See also Section 13.5.

actly the same idea—that evil has no *independent* existence—can
be found in the writings of 'Abdu'l-Bahá:

> As to thy remark, that 'Abdu'l-Bahá hath said to some
> of the believers that evil never exists, nay rather, it is
> a nonexistent thing, this is but truth, inasmuch as the
> greatest evil is man's going astray and being veiled from
> truth. Error is lack of guidance; darkness is absence of
> light; ignorance is lack of knowledge; falsehood is lack
> of truthfulness; blindness is lack of sight; and deafness
> is lack of hearing. Therefore, error, blindness, deafness
> and ignorance are nonexistent things.[11]

> ... it is possible that one thing in relation to another
> may be evil, and at the same time within the limits of
> its proper being it may not be evil. Then it is proved
> that there is no evil in existence; all that God created
> He created good. This evil is nothingness; so death is
> the absence of life. When man no longer receives life, he
> dies. Darkness is the absence of light: when there is no
> light, there is darkness. Light is an existing thing, but
> darkness is nonexistent. Wealth is an existing thing,
> but poverty is nonexisting. Then it is evident that
> all evils return to nonexistence. Good exists; evil is
> nonexistent.[12]

3.3 Theophanological Conflicts

The concept of the Manifestation of God is especially relevant today in relation to the conflicting views held by religious believers
about the Founders of their own particular Faith. Despite the
enormous energy devoted to theological pursuits—or perhaps because of it—there are today profound differences among Muslims
as to the precise station of Muhammad, among Christians as to
that of Jesus, and among Buddhists with respect to the Founder of
their own religion. Many of the world's religions have also sparred
with one another over the relative station of the Founders of their
own religion. Believers tend to believe that their own religion is
better than others'. For this reason, Bahá'u'lláh's detailed expla-

nations about the station of successive prophets are particularly interesting.

Every one of these Manifestations of God, Bahá'u'lláh says, has two stations: "the station of pure abstraction and essential unity," and "the station of distinction."[13] In the latter station, they are distinct servants of God. In the former station, they are all identically the Manifestation of God, equal in station. In the Kitáb-i-Íqán, Bahá'u'lláh writes:

> Were any of the all-embracing Manifestations of God to declare; "I am God," He, verily speaketh the truth, and no doubt attacheth thereto. For it hath been repeatedly demonstrated that through their Revelation, their attributes and names, the Revelation of God, His names and His attributes, are made manifest in the world... And were they all to proclaim, "I am the Seal of the Prophets," they, verily, utter but the truth, beyond the faintest shadow of doubt. For they are all but one person, one soul, one spirit, one being, one revelation. They are all the manifestation of the "Beginning" and the "End," the "First" and the "Last," the "Seen" and the "Hidden"—all of which pertain to Him Who is the Innermost Spirit of Spirits and Eternal Essence of Essences. And were they to say, "We are the Servants of God," this also is a manifest and indisputable fact. For they have been made manifest in the uttermost state of servitude, a servitude the like of which no man can possibly attain.[14]

Hence, most Bahá'ís can quite happily accept Jesus Christ as "the only begotten Son of God," Muhammad as "the Seal of the Prophets" (Khatam an-nabiyyin) and Krishna as "Supreme Spirit" (*Purushottama*) at one and the same time.[15] Bahá'ís do not see this view as inconsistent or contradictory because all these names and attributes are equally applicable to every Manifestation of God in "the station of pure abstraction and essential unity." From this point of view of "pure abstraction," Jesus, Krishna and Muhammad are all identically the same divine Being. All differences between them are attributable to their "station of distinction." Unfortunately, this point never seems to have been understood by most people. For example, while there is some overlap between the Hindu concept of *Avatara* and the Buddhist idea of Buddhahood, in general Buddhists do not accept Jesus or Muhammad as a Buddha. Similarly, Jews, Christians and Muslims do not accept the Buddha as a Prophet. Historically, a Christian who regarded Buddha and Jesus as equals ran the risk of being accused as heretic! From the Bahá'í and Gandhian points of view, such parochial religious exclusivism is unnecessary and runs against the true spirit of religion. Bahá'ís believe that the Manifestations of God are like different teachers in a school. All teachers have the same rank and station, but the level of the student changes with time. Thus, according to Bahá'í thinking, there is no fundamental difference between Moses, Zoroaster, Jesus or the Buddha when they are viewed in their "station of pure abstraction and essential unity." Their teachings differ only on account of the different requirements of the specific periods and places in which they lived. This explanation clarifies a number of issues relating to the founders of past religions.

Another example of the unifying power of concept of the Manifestation of God concerns beliefs about God. Whereas Judaism, Christianity and Islam are monotheistic faiths, Buddha preached a religion in which there is little or no mention of a Divine Being. Hence Buddhism has been regarded by many as an atheistic religion. How can monotheism be reconciled with atheism? Indeed, it cannot. It is fascinating to note, in this connection, what Gandhi and 'Abdu'l-Bahá had to say about the Buddha and belief in God. (Perhaps the reader can already infer that if "God is Truth," then disbelief in God must be inconsistent and irrational, since even atheists and Buddhists believe in truth.) 'Abdu'l-Bahá said,

> Buddha... established a new religion... The beliefs and rites of the Buddhists... have not continued in accordance with their fundamental teachings. The founder of Buddhism was a wonderful soul. He established the Oneness of God, but later the original principles of His doctrines gradually disappeared, and ignorant customs and ceremonials arose and increased until they finally ended in the worship of statues and

images.[16]

Gandhi held a similar view. In a speech delivered by Gandhi at
Vidyodaya College, Colombo, in reply to an address presented to
him by the All Ceylon Congress of Buddhist Associations, he said,

> I know that I speak in the presence of very learned
> priests and equally learned laymen, but I should be
> false to you and false to myself if I did not declare
> what my heart believes... I have heard it contended
> times without number and I have read in books also
> claiming to express the spirit of Buddhism that Bud-
> dha did not believe in God. In my humble opinion
> such a belief contradicts the very central fact of Bud-
> dha's teaching. In my humble opinion the confusion
> has arisen over his rejection and just rejection of all
> the base things that passed in his generation under the
> name of God. He undoubtedly rejected the notion that
> a being called God was actuated by malice, could re-
> pent of his actions, and like the kings of the earth could
> possibly have favorites. His whole soul rose in mighty
> indignation against the belief that a being called God
> required for his satisfaction the living blood of animals
> in order that he might be pleased, animals who were his
> own creation. He, therefore, reinstated God in the right
> place and dethroned the usurper who for the time being
> seemed to occupy that White Throne. He emphasized
> and redeclared the eternal and unalterable existence of
> the moral government of this universe... And hence
> the great confusion that Buddha disbelieved in God
> and simply believed in the moral law, and because of
> this confusion about God Himself, arose the confusion
> about the proper understanding of the great word *nir-
> vana*. *Nirvana* is undoubtedly not utter extinction. So
> far as I have been able to understand the central fact
> of Buddha's life, *nirvana* is utter extinction of all that
> is base in us, all that is vicious in us, all that is corrupt
> and corruptible in us. *Nirvana* is not like the black,
> dead peace of the grave, but the living peace, the liv-

ing happiness of a soul which is conscious of itself, and conscious of having found its own abode in the heart of the Eternal.[17]

It may interest the reader to know that most Bahá'ís would probably side with Gandhi as to the interpretation of *Nirvana:** the "death of self"[18] refers not to the extinction of self-reflective human consciousness, but rather to the complete and utter submission to the will of the Manifestation of God. Ego—not the "soul"—is extinguished. Indeed, in such a state, the seekers will see nothing in themselves, but see God in everything.

3.4 Oneness of Religion

If the Manifestations of God are all essentially a single Phenomenon, then their religions must also be essentially one and the same. This point is rather obvious, and it is a pity that the great majority of leaders of religions do not realize this truth even today. The following excerpts show that Gandhi believed strongly in the essential oneness of religion:

> In theory, since there is one God, there can be only one religion.[19]

> The soul of religions is one, but it is encased in a multitude of forms.[20]

> I believe in the fundamental truth of all great religions of the world. I believe that they are all God-given, and I believe that they were necessary for the people to whom these religions were revealed. And I believe that, if only we could all of us read the scriptures of the different faiths from the standpoint of the followers of those faiths, we should find that they were at the bottom all one and were all helpful to one another.[21]

> Religions are not for separating men from one another, they are meant to bind them.[21]

---

* *Nirvana* in Sanskrit literally means "extinction" or "blowing-out."

I do not believe in the exclusive divinity of the Vedas.
I believe the Bible, the Koran and the Zend Avesta to
be as much divinely inspired as the Vedas.[22]

I cannot ascribe exclusive divinity to Jesus. He is
as divine as Krishna or Rama or Mahomed [sic] or
Zoroaster... The Bible is as much a book of religion
with me as the Gita and the Koran.[23]

Bahá'ís believe, similarly, that religion is essentially a single
progressive process and that truth is to be found in all the major
world faiths. 'Abdu'l-Bahá advocates an inclusivist approach to
religion:

'Seek the truth, the truth shall make you free.' So shall
we see the truth in all religions, for truth is in all and
truth is one![24]

Religions, races, and nations are all divisions of man's
making only, and are necessary only in his thought;
before God there are neither Persians, Arabs, French
nor English; God is God for all, and to Him all creation
is one. We must obey God, and strive to follow Him
by leaving all our prejudices and bringing about peace
on earth.[25]

No one truth can contradict another truth. Light is
good in whatsoever lamp it is burning! A rose is beautiful in whatsoever garden it may bloom! A star has
the same radiance if it shines from the East or from
the West. Be free from prejudice, so will you love the
Sun of Truth from whatsoever point in the horizon it
may arise! You will realize that if the Divine light of
truth shone in Jesus Christ it also shone in Moses and
in Buddha. The earnest seeker will arrive at this truth.
This is what is meant by the 'Search after Truth'.[24]

... the establishing of the divine religions is for peace,
not for war and the shedding of blood. Inasmuch as all
are founded upon one reality which is love and unity,

the wars and dissensions which have characterized the
history of religion have been due to imitations and su-
perstitions which arise afterward. Religion is reality
and reality is one. The fundamentals of the religion
of God are therefore one in reality. There is neither
difference nor change in the fundamentals. Variance is
caused by blind imitations, prejudices and adherence
to forms which appear later, and inasmuch as these
differ, discord and strife result. If the religions of the
world would forsake these causes of difficulty and seek
the fundamentals, all would agree, and strife and dis-
sension would pass away; for religion and reality are
one and not multiple.[26]

All these holy, divine Manifestations are one. They
have served one God, promulgated the same truth,
founded the same institutions and reflected the same
light. Their appearances have been successive and correlated; each one has announced and extolled the one
who was to follow and all laid the foundation of reality. They summoned and invited the people to love and
made the human world a mirror of the Word of God.
Therefore the divine religions they established have one
foundation; their teachings, proofs and evidences are
one; in name and form they differ but in reality they
agree and are the same. These holy Manifestations
have been as the coming of springtime in the world.
Although the springtime of this year is designated by
another name according to the changing calendar, yet
as regards its life and quickening it is the same as the
springtime of last year. For each spring is the time of
a new creation, the effects, bestowals, perfections and
life-giving forces of which are the same as those of the
former vernal seasons although the names are many
and various. This is 1912, last year's was 1911 and so
on, but in fundamental reality no difference is apparent. The sun is one but the dawning-points of the sun
are numerous and changing. The ocean is one body of

water but different parts of it have particular designation, Atlantic, Pacific, Mediterranean, Antarctic, etc. If we consider the names, there is differentiation, but the water, the ocean itself is one reality. Likewise the divine religions of the holy Manifestations of God are in reality one though in name and nomenclature they differ. Man must be a lover of the light no matter from what day-spring it may appear. He must be a lover of the rose no matter in what soil it may be growing. He must be a seeker of the truth no matter from what source it come. Attachment to the lantern is not loving the light. Attachment to the earth is not befitting but enjoyment of the rose which develops from the soil is worthy. Devotion to the tree is profitless but partaking of the fruit is beneficial. Luscious fruits no matter upon what tree they grow or where they may be found must be enjoyed. The word of truth no matter which tongue utters it must be sanctioned. Absolute verities no matter in what book they be recorded must be accepted. If we harbor prejudice it will be the cause of deprivation and ignorance. The strife between religions, nations and races arises from misunderstanding. If we investigate the religions to discover the principles underlying their foundations we will find they agree, for the fundamental reality of them is one and not multiple. By this means the religionists of the world will reach their point of unity and reconciliation. They will ascertain the truth that the purpose of religion is the acquisition of praiseworthy virtues, betterment of morals, spiritual development of mankind, the real life and divine bestowals. All the prophets have been the promoters of these principles; none of them has been the promoter of corruption, vice or evil. They have summoned mankind to all good. They have united people in the love of God, invited them to the religions of the unity of mankind and exhorted them to amity and agreement.[27]

3.5 Progressive Revelation

Gandhi was a firm believer in the oneness of religion, but he does not appear to have believed in (or understood) the fundamentally evolutionary nature of religion.* In contrast, the progressive, evolutionary—and hence relative—nature of religion is a central idea in the teachings of the Bahá'í Faith.

Traces of the ideas of evolution and progression in religion can be found in the holy scriptures of most religions, including the Holy Bible, the Holy Quran, and the *Bhagavad Gita*. Bahá'u'lláh took the germ of the idea of evolution in religion, and transformed it into a central doctrine of the Bahá'í Faith by giving it a coherent formulation. Since Gandhi did not have a thorough knowledge of Bahá'u'lláh's teachings, it is not surprising that his understanding of this subject is not as fully developed. Indeed, this is one of the main differences between their views of religion. Nevertheless, Gandhi certainly did have some inkling of the concept:

> If we turn our eyes to the time of which history has any record down to our own time, we shall find that man has been steadily progressing towards ahimsa [nonviolence]. Our remote ancestors were cannibals. Then came a time when they were fed up with cannibalism and they began to live on chase. Next came a stage when man was ashamed of leading the life of a wandering hunter. He therefore took to agriculture and depended principally on mother earth for his food. Thus from being a nomad he settled down to a civilized stable life, founded villages and towns, and from member of a family he became member of a community and a nation. All these are signs of progressive ahimsa and diminishing himsa [violence]. Had it been otherwise, the human species should have been extinct by now, even as many of the lower species have disappeared.

> Prophets and avatars have also taught the lesson of ahimsa more or less. Not one of them has professed to teach ahimsa. And how should it be otherwise?

---

*See also Section 13.3.

Ahimsa does not need to be taught. Man as animal
is violent, but as Spirit is non-violent. The moment
he awakes to the Spirit within, he cannot remain violent. Either he progresses towards ahimsa or rushes to
his doom. That is why the prophets and avatars have
taught the lesson of truth, harmony, brotherhood, justice, etc.—all attributes of ahimsa.[28]

Consider, moreover, that Gandhi believed that Buddha's teachings
represented an advance over the then existing religions:

Buddha never rejected Hinduism, but he broadened its
base. He gave it a new life and a new interpretation.[29]

The Hindu religion underwent its first trial on the advent of Lord Buddha... At that time the Hindus were
under the glamour of the outward form of their religion,
and the *Brahmins* had, out of selfishness, abandoned
their true function of defending the Hindu faith. Lord
Buddha was moved to pity when he saw his religion
reduced to such a plight. He renounced the world and
started doing penance. He spent several years in devout
contemplation and ultimately suggested some reform in
the Hindu religion. His piety greatly affected the minds
of the *Brahmins,* and the killing of animals for sacrifice
was stopped to a great extent... We have seen that
Buddhism had a salutary effect on Hinduism, that the
champions of the latter were aroused by its impact.[30]

Unlike Bahá'ís, however, Gandhi did not understand that Buddha
meant to start a fundamentally new religion:

It cannot... be said that the Buddha founded a new or
different religion... It may be said that, in India at
any rate, Hinduism and Buddhism were but one, and
that even today the fundamental principles of both are
identical.[30]

Bahá'ís would agree that the fundamental spiritual principles of
all religions are the same. According to Bahá'í thinking, however,

the Buddha was not merely a religious reformer, but rather an independent Manifestation of God, the founder of a new religion with *distinct* social teachings different from those of the previous religions. (For example, Buddhism differs from the older Hindu religion on the subject of the caste system.)

If Gandhi can be thought of as having had some inkling about progressive religious revelation, then the Bahá'ís can be thought of as possessing an entire philosophical framework. Indeed a very significant fraction of the Bahá'í holy writings deal with the issue of progressive revelation. A thorough treatment of this subject is well beyond the scope of this book. The basic idea is that the "medicine" that is appropriate for today's social and spiritual "sickness" need not be the same medicine prescribed during a previous era, because each sickness has its own special remedy. Bahá'u'lláh explains that religion is "revealed" by God according to the evolutionary level of civilization:

> O people! Words are revealed according to capacity so that the beginners may make progress. The milk must be given according to measure so that the babe of the world may enter into the Realm of Grandeur and be established in the Court of Unity.[31]

Esslemont explains this idea further:

> It is milk that strengthens the babe so that it can digest more solid food later on. To say that because one Prophet is right in giving a certain teaching at a certain time, therefore another Prophet must be wrong Who gives a different teaching at a different time, is like saying that because milk is the best food for the newborn babe, therefore, milk and nothing but milk should be the food of the grown man also, and to give any other diet would be wrong![32]

> God is the great Physician Who alone can rightly diagnose the world's sickness and prescribe the appropriate remedy. The remedy prescribed in one age is no longer suitable in a later age, when the condition of the patient

is different. To cling to the old remedy when the physician has ordered new treatment is not to show faith in the physician, but infidelity. It may be a shock to the Jew to be told that some of the remedies for the world's sickness which Moses ordered over three thousand years ago are now out of date and unsuitable; the Christian may be equally shocked when told that Muhammad had anything necessary or valuable to add to what Jesus prescribed; and so also the Muslim, when asked to admit that the Báb or Bahá'u'lláh had authority to alter the commands of Muhammad; but according to the Bahá'í view, true devotion to God implies reverence to all His Prophets, and implicit obedience to His latest Commands, as given by the Prophet for our own age. Only by such devotion can true Unity be attained.[33]

Complementing the view that there is only one religion since there is only one God is the idea that this eternal religion is expressed through changing forms. For while the religion of God is the One Religion, on the other hand it is a living and a growing thing, not lifeless and unchanging. Bahá'ís see in the teaching of Moses or Krishna the Bud, in that of Christ or Buddha the Flower, in that of Bahá'u'lláh the Fruit, and after Bahá'u'lláh there will be other Manifestations of God. Indeed, the flower does not destroy the bud, nor does the fruit destroy the flower—rather the bud evolves into the fruit. 'Abdu'l-Bahá explains this concept further:

Each divine revelation is divided into two parts. The first part is essential and belongs to the eternal world. It is the exposition of Divine truths and essential principles. It is the expression of the Love of God. This is one in all the religions, unchangeable and immutable. The second part is not eternal; it deals with practical life, transactions and business, and changes according to the evolution of man and the requirements of the time of each Prophet. For example... During the Mosaic period the hand of a person was cut off in punishment of a small theft; there was a law of an eye for an eye and a tooth for a tooth, but as these laws were not expedient in the time of Christ, they were abrogated. Likewise divorce had become so universal that there remained no fixed laws of marriage, therefore His Holiness Christ forbade divorce. According to the exigencies of the time, His Holiness Moses revealed ten laws for capital punishment. It was impossible at that time to protect the community and to preserve social security without these severe measures, for the children of Israel lived in the wilderness of Tah, where there were no established courts of justice and no penitentiaries. But this code of conduct was not needed in the time of Christ. The history of the second part of religion is unimportant, because it relates to the customs of this life only; but the foundation of the religion of God is one, and His Holiness Bahá'u'lláh has renewed that foundation.[34]

Bahá'u'lláh gave a detailed prescription for healing today's social, economic, and spiritual problems; the central theme is unity. Bahá'u'lláh declares further:

That which the Lord hath ordained as the sovereign remedy and mightiest instrument for the healing of all the world is the union of all its peoples in one universal Cause, one common Faith. This can in no wise be achieved except through the power of a skilled, an all-powerful and inspired Physician.[31]

Chapter Notes

1. See the Bahá'í Long Obligatory Prayer. Bahá'u'lláh commands the Bahá'ís to pray at least daily. The Bahá'ís are free to chose one of the three prayers specifically revealed for this purpose. The Long Obligatory Prayer is the longest of the three. For the text of the prayer, see *Kitáb-i-Aqdas* (Haifa: Bahá'í World Centre, 1992), 93–9.

2. *The Gospel of Selfless Action or The Gita According to Gandhi.* Ed. Mahadev Desai (Ahmedabad: Navajivan Publishing House, 1984), 319.

3. *All Men Are Brothers: Life and Thoughts of Mahatma Gandhi as Told in His Own Words.* Ed. K Kripalani (Paris: UNESCO, 1969), 63.

4. *All Men Are Brothers*, 58.

5. *All Men Are Brothers*, 71.

6. *Gleanings from the Writings of Bahá'u'lláh.* (Wilmette: Bahá'í Publishing Trust, 1976), 3–5. Trans. Shoghi Effendi.

7. *Gleanings from the Writings of Bahá'u'lláh*, 47–48.

8. *The Gospel of Selfless Action or The Gita According to Gandhi*, 128.

9. *Bhagavad Gita* Book IV, verse 6.

10. *The Gita According to Gandhi*, 196.

11. 'Abdu'l-Bahá, quoted in J. E. Esslemont, *Bahá'u'lláh and the New Era*, 5th rev. ed. (Wilmette: Bahá'í Publishing Trust, 1987), 195–6.

12. *Some Answered Questions.* (Wilmette: Bahá'í Publishing Trust, 1990), 264.

13. *Gleanings from the Writings of Bahá'u'lláh*, 50–2.

14. *Gleanings from the Writings of Bahá'u'lláh*, 54.

15. Bahá'u'lláh explains that names and attributes like "Supreme Being," "Son of God" and "final prophet," among others, can become "veils" that conceal God. These veils prevent the followers of religions from recognizing Truth in the religions of others. Hence, animosity continually prevails between the religions, because human beings allow such names and attributes to becomes the cause of confusion and disunity. See for example: John 3:16 in the Holy Bible; Surah Al Ahzab 40 in the Holy Quran; *Bhagavad Gita* 10:15.

16. *Some Answered Questions,* 195.

17. M. K. Gandhi, *In Search of the Supreme. Volume Three.* Ed. V. B. Kher (Ahmedabad: Navajivan press, 1962), 295.

18. The "death of self" is a theme that is found in Sufi literature and in some of the writings of Bahá'u'lláh and corresponds to similar ideas in other religions, e.g., *nirvana, moksha,* and "union with God." See also Bahá'u'lláh's *The Seven Valleys and the Four Valleys* (Wilmette: Bahá'í Publishing Trust, 1991).

19. *The Mind of Mahatma Gandhi.* Ed. R. K. Prabhu and U. R. Rao (Ahmedabad: Navajivan Publishing House, 1967), 67.

20. *The Mind of Mahatma Gandhi,* 66.

21. *The Mind of Mahatma Gandhi,* 67–8.

22. M. K. Gandhi, Aspects of Hinduism, in *Hindu Dharma* (New Delhi: Orient Paperbacks, 1987), 9–10

23. *The Mind of Mahatma Gandhi,* 98.

24. *Paris Talks* (London: Bahá'í Publishing Trust, 1972), 137.

25. *Paris Talks,* 131.

26. *Foundations of World Unity* (Wilmette: Bahá'í Publishing Trust, 1979), 23.

27. *Foundations of World Unity,* 23.

28. *All Men Are Brothers,* 86–87.

29. *In Search of the Supreme. Volume Three,* 294.

30. *The Essential Writings of Mahatma Gandhi.* Ed. Raghavan Iyer (Oxford: Oxford University Press, 1990), 139–40.

31. Bahá'u'lláh, quoted in *Bahá'u'lláh and the New Era,* 122.

32. *Bahá'u'lláh and the New Era,* 123.

33. *Bahá'u'lláh and the New Era,* 125.

34. 'Abdu'l-Bahá, quoted in *Bahá'u'lláh and the New Era,* 123.

Chapter 4

Prayer and Fasting

In Western Medicine there is a phenomenon known as the "placebo effect." Even when an unsuspecting patient is prescribed sugar pills instead of medicine, still the patient sometimes reports that symptoms improve. In other words, the mere belief that the pills—made of sugar that has no pharmacological value—will help leads to an improvement in the condition of the individual. This is a remarkable phenomenon whose full significance has until recently not been fully appreciated by the medical community. Stripped to its essentials, it suggests that *faith can heal*. Traditionally, in Western Medicine, this effect was considered a nuisance whose effect had to be subtracted from clinical drug tests. Hence to this day "double blind" tests are conducted in which neither patient nor doctor can distinguish the patients prescribed the real drugs apart from those given the placebos. Fortunately, even secular society is slowly opening up to the use of meditation, prayer, etc. A very encouraging development is that recently, the medical community has begun to realize the relevance of an individual's beliefs to health. For example, a research team at Harvard Medical School conducted tests to study the effects of prayer on the health of patients.[1]

Why study prayer, and what does the placebo effect have to do with it? When people supplicate God for health, they are implicitly placing their faith—trusting their beliefs—in the power of prayer. Indeed, prayer is a potent means of accessing and altering our innermost beliefs. Fasting has similarly been used for tens of thousands of years as a complement to prayer. Moreover, prayer and fasting can lead to slightly altered states of consciousness in which the material world becomes less important, thereby opening our minds to the subtler—more spiritual—aspects of our existence. The power of prayer is not limited to matters of health, however. Through mechanisms as yet not properly understood by science, prayer and fasting seem to be able to release disproportionately large forces. Priests, shamans, politicians, healers and spiritualists of all ages have made liberal use of prayer and fasting for thousands of years. Basically, prayer and fasting are two of the most basic tools of the "art" and "science" of spiritual transformation.

In our age, prayer and fasting have become less important, even empty rituals in some sad cases. But if we sincerely aspire to build a new kind of civilization based on collective security, nonviolence, and spiritual values, then it would be unconscionable to neglect the value of prayer, meditation, deep contemplation, and fasting. Ultimately, we need to change people's hearts, so every attempt to build a better, nonviolent civilization will fail if matters of the heart and of the spirit are neglected.

This chapter examines prayer and fasting as understood by Gandhi and by the Bahá'ís. Gandhi made effective use of prayer and fasting—indeed, his fasts attained worldwide fame. Prayer and fasting are also integral aspects of the life-pattern in the Bahá'í community. Bahá'ís pray at least daily. They also fast from sunrise to sunset, abstaining from all food and drink, for a period of 19 days that ends every year with the Bahá'í New Year Festival of Naw Rúz. The Bahá'í New Year, like the ancient Persian New Year, is astronomically fixed to coincide with the March equinox (usually March 21). The Bahá'í fast is not binding on children, pregnant or nursing mothers, travelers, or on those who are too old or too weak.

4.1   Need for Prayer

Gandhi believed that Truth is God and the Bahá'í writings often refer to God as the "Sun of Truth."* As the physical sun provides nourishing energy to the physical earth, so does the Sun of Truth provide nourishment to the earth of our hearts. Gandhi considers prayer to be a form of communion with the Spirit of Truth:

> This God whom we seek to realize is Truth. Or to put it another way Truth is God. This Truth is not merely the truth we are expected to speak. It is that which alone is, which constitutes the stuff of which all things are made, which subsists by virtue of its own power, which is not supported by anything else but supports everything that exists. Truth alone is eternal, everything else is momentary. It need not assume shape or form. It is pure intelligence as well as pure bliss. We call it [God] because everything is regulated by Its will. It and the law it promulgates are one. Therefore it is not a blind law. It governs the entire universe. To propitiate this Truth is [prayer] which in effect means an earnest desire to be filled with the spirit of Truth. This desire should be present all the twenty-four hours. But our souls are too dull to have this awareness day and night. Therefore we offer prayers for a short time in the hope that a time will come when all our conduct will be one continuously sustained prayer.[2]

Gandhi further explains that prayer is a means of freeing us form excessive attachment to the material world:

> I agree that, if man could practice the presence of God all the twenty-four hours, there would be no need for a separate time for prayer. But most people find this impossible. The sordid everyday world is too much with them. For them the practice of complete withdrawal of the mind from all outward things, even though it might be only for a few minutes everyday, will be found to be of infinite use. Silent communion will help them to experience an undisturbed peace in the midst of turmoil, to curb anger and cultivate patience.[3]

---

*See also Chapters 2,3

Not only is it a means to become more detached from the trappings of this world, but people also crave closeness to the True Beloved of their hearts. Hence, prayer serves not only to make us more detached, but also to bind us more tightly to the Source of our spiritual life. Prayer is the language of love. 'Abdu'l-Bahá explains:

> If one friend loves another, is it not natural that he should wish to say so? Though he knows that that friend is aware of his love, does he still not wish to tell him of it? ... It is true that God knows the wishes of all hearts; but the impulse to pray is a natural one, springing from man's love to God... Prayer need not be in words, but rather in thought and action. But if this love and this desire are lacking, it is useless to try to force them. Words without love mean nothing. If a person talks to you as an unpleasant duty, finding neither love nor enjoyment in the meeting, do you wish to converse with him?

As the above passages suggest, the human mind is intrinsically attracted to truth and beauty. It can be argued that human beings are instinctively drawn to prayer.[1] From this point of view, prayer is as necessary for our spiritual health as food is necessary for the body. Gandhi explains concisely:

> As food is necessary for the body, prayer is necessary for the soul.[4]

Bahá'u'lláh echoes this theme in a prayer:

> O my Lord! Make Thy beauty to be my food, and Thy presence my drink...[5]

4.2 Conversation with God

According to 'Abdu'l-Bahá, prayer is "conversation with God."[6] He explains further:

> We must strive to attain to that condition by being separated from all things and from the people of the

world and by turning to God alone. It will take some
effort on the part of man to attain to that condition,
but he must work for it, strive for it. We can attain to
it by thinking and caring less for material things and
more for the spiritual. The further we go from the one,
the nearer we are to the other. The choice is ours. Our
spiritual perception, our inward sight must be opened,
so that we can see the signs and traces of God's spirit
in everything. Everything can reflect to us the light of
the Spirit.[7]

Gandhi held similar views on prayer. He explains the devotional
attitude as follows:

True meditation consists in closing the eyes and ears
of the mind to all else, except the object of one's devotion.[8]

In heartfelt prayer the worshipper's attention is concen-
trated on the object of worship so much so that he is
not conscious of anything else besides. The worshipper
has well been compared to a lover. The lover forgets
the whole world and even himself in the presence of the
beloved. The identification of the worshipper with God
should be closer still...[9]

4.3 Power of Prayer

Neither Gandhi nor the Bahá'ís underestimate the power of prayer.
Gandhi believed that the power of prayer is very great indeed:

Supplication, worship, prayer are no superstition; they
are acts more real than the acts of eating, drinking,
sitting or walking. It is no exaggeration to say that
they alone are real, all else is unreal.[10]

God answers prayer in His own way, not ours. His ways
are different from the ways of mortals. Hence they are
inscrutable. Prayer presupposes faith. No prayer goes

in vain. Prayer is like any other action. It bears fruit
whether we see it or not, and the fruit of heart prayer
[sic] is far more potent than action so-called.[11]

Bahá'ís believe that the power of prayer is very great because the
source of the power is none other than God. Esslemont explains
concisely:

> If a magnet be held over some iron filings the latter will
> fly upwards and cling to it, but this involves no inter-
> ference with the law of gravitation. The force of gravity
> continues to act on the filings just as before. What has
> happened is that a superior force has been brought into
> play—another force whose action is just as regular and
> calculable as that of gravity. The Bahá'í view is that
> prayer brings into action higher forces, as yet compara-
> tively little known; but there seems no reason to believe
> that these forces are more arbitrary in their action than
> the physical forces. The difference is that they have not
> yet been fully studied and experimentally investigated,
> and their action appears mysterious and incalculable
> because of our ignorance... A small force, when ap-
> plied to the sluice gate of a reservoir, may release and
> regulate an enormous flow of water-power, or, when
> applied to the steering gear of an ocean liner, may con-
> trol the course of the huge vessel. In the Bahá'í view,
> the power that brings about answers to prayer is the
> inexhaustible Power of God. The part of the suppli-
> ant is only to exert the feeble force necessary to release
> the flow or determine the course of the Divine Bounty,
> which is ever ready to serve those who have learned
> how to draw upon it.[12]

4.4 Nature of Fasting

According to both Gandhi and the Bahá'í Faith, the purpose of
fasting is to bring us closer to God. 'Abdu'l-Bahá explains:

> Fasting is a symbol. Fasting signifies abstinence from

lust. Physical fasting is a symbol of that abstinence, and is a reminder; that is, just as a person abstains from physical appetites, he is to abstain from self-appetites and self-desires. But mere abstention from food has no effect on the spirit. It is only a symbol, a reminder. Otherwise it is of no importance. Fasting for this purpose does not mean entire abstinence from food. The golden rule as to food is, do not take too much or too little. Moderation is necessary. There is a sect in India who practice extreme abstinence, and gradually reduce their food until they exist on almost nothing. But their intelligence suffers. A man is not fit to do service for God with brain or body if he is weakened by lack of food. He cannot see clearly.[13]

Some of these ideas can also be found in the writings of Gandhi:

A genuine fast cleanses the body, mind and soul. It crucifies the flesh and to that extent sets the soul free. A sincere prayer can work wonders. It is an intense longing of the soul for its even greater purity. Purity thus gained, when it is utilized for a noble purpose, becomes prayer.[14]

I believe that there is no prayer without fasting, and there is no real fast without prayer.[14]

I know that the mental attitude is everything. Just as prayer may be merely a mechanical intonation as of a bird, so may a fast be a mere mechanical torture of the flesh... Neither will touch the soul.[14]

4.5 ⁄ Prayer in Action

Prayer implies a life of service to others. We can be of service to God in no other way, for if we turn our backs on others, are we not turning our backs upon God? 'Abdu'l-Bahá stated emphatically:

This is worship: to serve mankind and to minister to the needs of the people. Service is prayer. A physician

ministering to the sick, gently, tenderly, free from prejudice and believing in the solidarity of the human race,
is giving praise.[15]

Gandhi, too, was very much aware of this truth:

There is no worship purer or more pleasing to God than
selfless service of the poor.[16]

Chapter Notes

1. Dr. Herbert Benson at Harvard Medical School is a pioneer in be-
havioral medicine and mind-body studies, as well as in spirituality
and healing. Through his work, he defined the "relaxation response"
and continues to lead reasearch into its efficacy in counteracting the
harmful effects of stress. The relaxation response is a meditative
process which interrupts the sympathetic nervous system's storm
of the fight-flight reaction, and is taught as a form of prayer for
persons from religious traditions, while for the non-religious it is
taught as a form of meditation. The two general steps to eliciting the relaxation response are (i) to repeat a word, sound, prayer,
phrase, or muscular activity and (ii) to disregard everyday thoughts
that come to mind, and passively return to the repetition. There are
nine specific steps that seem to work well for eliciting the relaxation
response: (1) pick a focus word or prayer that is rooted in your belief system; (2) sit quietly in a comfortable position; (3) close your
eyes; (4) relax your muscles; (5) breathe slowly and naturally, and
repeat the chosen focus word, phrase, or prayer silently to yourself
while exhaling; (6) if other thoughts come to mind, gently and passively return to the repetition; (7) continue the repetiton for ten to
twenty minutes; (8) do not stand immediately, rather sit quietly for
about a minute, allowing other thoughts to return before opening
your eyes and then slowly rising; (9) practice this technique once or
twice daily. Secular focus words can include, e.g., "Ocean," "Love,"
"Peace," "Calm," and "Relax." Religious focus words or prayers
can include, e.g., "Our Father who art in heaven" for Christians,
"Shalom" and "The Lord is my shepherd" for Jews, "Inshallah"
for Muslims, "Om" for Hindus and Buddhists, and "Alláh'u'Abhá"
(God the Most Glorious) for Bahá'ís. Dr. Benson and others have
used the relaxation response to treat hypertension, anxiety, chronic
pain, and heart disease in a general program of stress management,
and have scientifically shown that prayer is good for the person
who prays. Moreover, in his recent book, Benson goes so far as to
say that we're wired for God, meaning that faith is a survival trait
that is biologically built into human beings. See Herbert Benson,
Timeless Healing: The Power and Biology of Belief (New York:
Scribner, 1996).

2. M. K. Gandhi, *In Search of the Supreme. Volume One.* Ed. V. B.
Kher (Ahmedabad: Navajivan press, 1962), 196.

3. *The Mind of Mahatma Gandhi*. Ed. R. K. Prabhu and U. R. Rao (Ahmedabad: Navajivan Publishing House, 1967), 88.

4. *The Mind of Mahatma Gandhi*, 87.

5. *Prayers and Meditations by Bahá'u'lláh*. Trans. Shoghi Effendi (Wilmette: Bahá'í Publishing Trust, 1987), 261.

6. 'Abdu'l-Bahá, quoted in J. E. Esslemont, *Bahá'u'lláh and the New Era*, 5th rev. ed. (Wilmette: Bahá'í Publishing Trust, 1987), 88.

7. 'Abdu'l-Bahá, quoted in *Bahá'u'lláh and the New Era*, 89.

8. *In Search of the Supreme. Volume One*, 221.

9. *In Search of the Supreme. Volume One*, 197.

10. *The Mind of Mahatma Gandhi*, 86.

11. *The Mind of Mahatma Gandhi*, 91.

12. *Bahá'u'lláh and the New Era*, 97.

13. 'Abdu'l-Bahá, quoted in *Bahá'u'lláh and the New Era*, 184.

14. *The Mind of Mahatma Gandhi*, 35.

15. 'Abdu'l-Bahá, quoted in *Bahá'u'lláh and the New Era*, 79.

16. *In Search of the Supreme. Volume One*, 147.

Chapter 5

The Power of Nonviolence

One of the first people to mention nonviolence in a broad social context was the Buddha (Siddhartha Gautama, circa 563–483 B.C.E.). He spoke at length about nonviolence, but only some centuries later did the idea percolate into Indian civilization. Nonviolence is the English word used by Gandhi and others for *Ahimsa*, the Sanskrit antonym of *himsa*, which means "hurt" or "harm." The idea of nonviolence is simple: not to hurt or harm. Nonviolence implicitly includes the "golden rule" which says that we should not treat others as we would not wish to be treated.

It is clear even from the word's etymology that a civilization that is not based on nonviolence will *ipso facto* generate violence— hence, pain, suffering, etc. This is why it is morally imperative that we collectively strive to reconstruct society along nonviolent principles. This chapter introduces the reader to the power and use of nonviolence, according to Gandhi and to the Bahá'ís.

5.1 Superior to Violence

According to Darwinian theories of evolution, it usually makes more sense to kill than to be killed, because it is not possible for a dead individual to procreate and to have offspring. This is certainly true of our animal aspect, but humans are more than animals. We are thinking, intelligent beings, capable of creating not only biological offspring but also poetry, music, ideas, theories, social movements, etc. The act of creation, after all, is not limited to the act of procreation! Hence, it is sometimes possible that a person can create more through physical death than through staying alive. Human history celebrates the lives of those who sacrificed their lives for a greater cause. Gandhi and Martin Luther King Jr. are recent examples of people who, though dead, continue to exert an influence as though still alive. Their lives attest to the truth that it can sometimes be better to be killed than to kill. More generally, it can be better to suffer harm than to hurt others. This truth captures the essential idea underlying the principle of nonviolence.

Gandhi is famous for his emphasis on nonviolence. He even felt that violent methods are unbecoming of intelligent human beings:

> Non-violence is the law of our species as violence is the law of the brute.[1]

> There is nothing very wonderful in killing and being killed in the process. But the man who offers his neck to the enemy for execution, but refuses to bend to his will, shows courage of a far higher type.[2]

The concept of nonviolence is also emphasized in the Bahá'í Faith and can be traced to its earliest days. Some years after the 1850 public execution of the Báb by firing-squad,* Bahá'u'lláh emerged as the leader of the new Faith and began to teach the surviving believers that "if ye be slain, it is better for you than to slay."[3] By 1863, when the Bahá'í Faith was founded by Bahá'u'lláh, the Bábí believers—now called Bahá'ís—had become distinctly nonviolent in their ethics as well as in their methods. Shoghi Effendi concisely sums up this change in direction in the following sentence taken from *God Passes By*, his masterpiece history of the first Bahá'í century:

> The dissociation of the Bábí Faith from every form of political activity and from all secret associations and

---

*See Section 1.1.

factions; *the emphasis placed on the principle of nonviolence;** the necessity of strict obedience to established authority; the ban imposed on all forms of sedition, on back-biting, retaliation, and dispute; the stress laid on godliness, kindliness, humility and piety, on honesty and truthfulness, chastity and fidelity, on justice, toleration, sociability, amity and concord, on the acquisition of arts and sciences, on self-sacrifice and detachment, on patience, steadfastness and resignation to the will of God—all these constitute the salient features of a code of ethical conduct to which the books, treatises and epistles, revealed during those years, by the indefatigable pen of Bahá'u'lláh, unmistakably bear witness.[4]

Violence, oppression, tyranny are all categorically and repeatedly condemned in the Bahá'í writings. 'Abdu'l-Bahá explains that while violent methods might have been tolerable in earlier stages of human evolution, now we are more mature and have no excuse to resort to violence:

O ye lovers of God! In this, the cycle of Almighty God, violence and force, constraint and oppression, are one and all condemned.[5]

There are many other instances where nonviolence is emphasized in the Bahá'í Faith. For example, in the opening page of the 1976 edition of Esslemont's book, *Bahá'u'lláh and the New Era*, we read that the Bahá'í Faith takes "firm worldly positions in vital areas affecting modern man," including "Nonviolent Means."[6]

5.2   A Cohesive Force

It may be difficult for many people to accept that nonviolence is really superior to violence, for old ways of thinking die hard. One of the reasons why the power of nonviolence and compassion has been historically underestimated is that they are creative, cohesive

---

*Italics added.

forces—difficult to notice. In contrast, violence and hatred are destructive and repulsive forces, hence trivial to understand—every murderer can be considered an expert. It is quite instructive, if not amazing, to compare the views of 'Abdu'l-Bahá and of Gandhi on this subject. Gandhi writes:

> Scientists tell us that, without the presence of the cohesive force amongst the atoms that comprise this globe of ours, it would crumble to pieces and we would cease to exist; and even as there is cohesive force in blind matter, so must there be in all things animate, and the name for that cohesive force among animate beings is Love. We notice it between father and son, between brother and sister, friend and friend. But we have to learn to use that force among all that lives, and in the use of it consists our knowledge of God. Where there is love there is life; hatred leads to destruction.[7]

> The fact that mankind persists shows that the cohesive force is greater than the disruptive force...[8]

> The force of love is the same as the force of the soul or truth. We have evidence of its working at every step. The universe would disappear without the existence of that force...[9]

> Though there is repulsion in Nature, she *lives* by attraction. Mutual love enables nature to persist. Man does not live by destruction. Self-love compels regard for others. Nations cohere because there is mutual regard among individuals composing them. Some day, we must extend the national law to the universe, even as we have extended the family law to form nations—a larger family.[10]

'Abdu'l-Bahá writes on the same subject:

> Love is the most great law that ruleth this mighty and heavenly cycle, the unique power that bindeth together the divers elements of this material world, the supreme

magnetic force that directeth the movements of the
spheres in the celestial realms. Love revealeth with
unfailing and limitless power the mysteries latent in
the universe. Love is the spirit of life unto the adorned
body of mankind, the establisher of true civilization
in this mortal world, and the shedder of imperishable
glory upon every high-aiming race and nation.[11]

Therefore attraction and composition between the various elements is the means of life, and discord, decomposition and division produce death. Thus the cohesive
and attractive forces in all things lead to the appear-
ance of fruitful results and effects, while estrangement
and alienation of things lead to disturbance and annihi-
lation. Through affinity and attraction all living things
like plants, animals and men come into existence, while
division and discord bring about decomposition and destruction. Consequently, that which is conducive to association and attraction and unity among the sons of
men is the means of the life of the world of humanity,
and whatever causeth division, repulsion and remoteness leadeth to the death of humankind.[12]

5.3 A Creative Power

Since nonviolence is a creative rather than destructive power,
therefore it allows individuals and communities who draw upon it
to prosper spiritually relative to those that are ignorant of it. Until
now, the power of nonviolence has not been fully appreciated by the
majority of humankind. Hence people consider it extraordinary—
almost miraculous—that the Bahá'í Faith nonviolently withstood
the concerted and violent efforts of the Persian and Ottoman Empires to destroy it, or that Gandhi obtained independence for his
native land without armies. It is perhaps a sign of the times that
people consider it surprising that nonviolent, creative, energies can
overcome the destructive furies of violence.

Gandhi believed that nonviolent methods are inherently more
powerful than violence:

The fact is that non-violence does not work in the same way as violence. It works in the opposite way. An armed man naturally relies upon his arms. A man who is intentionally unarmed relies upon the Unseen Force called God by poets, but called the Unknown by scientists. But that which is unknown is not necessarily non-existent. God is the Force among all forces known and unknown. Non-violence without reliance upon that Force is poor stuff to be thrown in the dust.[13]

Non-violence is an active force of the highest order. It is soul force or the power of Godhead within us. Imperfect man cannot grasp the whole of that Essence—he would not be able to bear its full blaze, but even an infinitesimal fraction of of it, when it becomes active within us, can work wonders. The sun in the heavens fills the whole universe with its life-giving warmth. But if one went too near it, it would consume him to ashes. Even so it is with Godhead. We become Godlike to the extent we realize non-violence; but we can never become wholly God.[14]

This idea that what Gandhi calls "soul force" can produce apparently incredible results is a constant theme in the Bahá'í writings. Bahá'u'lláh writes concerning the nonviolent response of the Bahá'ís towards their oppressors:

Gracious God! This people need no weapons of destruction, inasmuch as they have girded themselves to reconstruct the world. Their hosts are the hosts of goodly deeds, and their arms the arms of upright conduct, and their commander the fear of God. Blessed that one that judgeth with fairness. By the righteousness of God! Such hath been the patience, the calm, the resignation of contentment of this people that they have become the exponents of justice, and so great hath been their forbearance, that they have suffered themselves to be killed rather than kill, and this notwithstanding that these whom the world hath wronged have

endured tribulations the like of which the history of the
world hath never recorded, nor the eyes of any nation
witnessed. What is it that could have induced them
to reconcile themselves to these grievous trials, and to
refuse to put forth a hand to repel them? What could
have caused such resignation and serenity? The true
cause is to be found in the ban which the Pen of Glory
hath, day and night, chosen to impose, and in Our assumption of the reins of authority, through the power
and might of Him Who is the Lord of all mankind.[15]

'Abdu'l-Bahá implies that the use of nonviolent methods is not as
difficult as it may appear to be:

Be self-sacrificing in the path of God, and wing thy
flight unto the heavens of the love of the Abhá Beauty,
for any movement animated by love moveth from the
periphery to the centre, from space to the Day-Star
of the universe. Perchance thou deemest this to be
difficult, but I tell thee that such cannot be the case,
for when the motivating and guiding power is the divine
force of magnetism it is possible, by its aid, to traverse
time and space easily and swiftly.[16]

Esslemont further explains the apparently paradoxical power of
nonviolence:

The soundness of Bahá'u'lláh's nonresistance policy
has already been proved by results. For every believer
martyred in Persia, the Bahá'í faith has received a hundred new believers into its fold, and the glad and daunt-
less way in which these martyrs cast the crowns of their
lives at the feet of their Lord has furnished to the world
the clearest proof that they had found a new life for
which death has no terrors, a life of ineffable fullness
and joy, compared with which the pleasures of earth
are but as dust in the balance, and the most fiendish
physical tortures but trifles light as air.[17]

5.4   Nonviolent Power Structures

Nonviolence can be artfully employed in the life of the individual, but its greatest effect is to be seen on our collective community lives. Since excessive centralization of political and economic power necessarily involves some degree of violence towards those in the periphery of society, therefore a nonviolent civilization must be based upon decentralized power structures. Gandhi explains:

> All society is held together by non-violence, even as the earth is held in her position by gravitation. But when the law of gravitation was discovered, the discovery yielded results of which our ancestors had no knowledge. Even so, when society is deliberately constructed in accordance with the law of non-violence, its structure will be different in material particulars from what it is today.[18]

> Centralization as a system is inconsistent with nonviolent structure of society.[19]

> What I would personally prefer would be not a centralization of power in the hands of the State, but an extention of the sense of trusteeship, as, in my opinion, the violence of private ownership is less injurious than the violence of the State. However, if that is unavoidable, I would support a minimum of state ownership.[20]

Similar ideas occur in the writings of 'Abdu'l-Bahá:

> It is very evident that in the future there shall be no centralization in the countries of the world, be they constitutional in government, republican or democratic in form. The United States may be held up as the example of future government—that is to say, each province will be independent in itself, but there will be federal union protecting the interests of the various independent states. It may not be a republican or a democratic form. To cast aside centralization which promotes despotism is the exigency of the time. This will be productive of international peace.[21]

5.5 Nonviolent Administration

In our contemporary civilization, social order is maintained because disobedience of the law leads to punishment: fines, prison terms, even capital punishment for serious crimes. This arrangement is not without its drawbacks, however. So long as people think they will not "get caught" or punished, they may convince themselves that there is nothing to be lost in breaking the law. Have not even many heads of state and of government in various countries attempted to break the law with impunity? Has today's civilization been able to proclaim victory over drug abuse, forced prostitution, smuggling, or environmental crimes? No sooner are new laws enacted than the "criminals" find new loopholes. Indeed, so long as we do not get caught or punished, it pays to commit crimes in our civilization.

Is there not a better method of ensuring social order that is based on the application of nonviolent spiritual principles? Both Gandhi and the Bahá'ís believe that a nonviolent, approach to social order is indeed possible. Gandhi explains:

> The principles on which a non-violent organization is based are different from and the reverse of what obtains in a violent organization. For instance, in the orthodox army, there is a clear distinction made between an officer and a private. The latter is subordinate and inferior to the former. In a non-violent army, the general is just the chief servant—first among equals. He claims no privilege over or superiority to the rank and file...

> The second difference between a military organization and a peace organization is that in the former the rank and file have no part in the choice of their general and their officers. These are imposed upon them and enjoy unrestricted power over them. In a non-violent army, the general and the officers are elected or are as if elected when their authority is moral and rests solely on the willing obedience of the rank and file.[22]

It may interest the reader to note that both these principles can be found put into practice in the Bahá'í community. All administrative authority is vested in elected consultative institutions at the local, national, and international levels. Individual members of such bodies have no authority and do not enjoy extra powers, but rather typically consider themselves fortunate to have been chosen to serve.

Regarding nonviolent law enforcement, Gandhi writes further:

> ... I have concluded that even in a non-violent State a police force may be necessary... The police of my conception will, however, be of a wholly different pattern from the present-day force. Its ranks will be composed of believers in non-violence. They will be servants, not masters, of the people. The people will instinctively render them every help, and through mutual cooperation they will easily deal with the ever-decreasing disturbances. The police force will have some kind of arms, but they will be rarely used, if at all. In fact the policemen will be reformers. Their police work will be confined primarily to robbers and dacoits. Quarrels between labour and capital and strikes will be few and far between in a non-violent state, because the influence of the non-violent majority will be so great as to command the respect of the principal elements in society. Similarly there will be no room for communal disturbances.[23]

'Abdu'l-Bahá also addressed the subject of law enforcement:

> ... communities must punish the oppressor, the murderer, the malefactor, so as to warn and restrain others from committing like crimes. But the most essential thing is that the people must be educated in such a way that no crimes will be committed; for it is possible to educate the masses so effectively that they will avoid and shrink from perpetrating crimes, so that the crime itself will appear to them as the greatest chastisement, the utmost condemnation and torment. Therefore, no crimes which require punishment will be committed...
>
> ... communities are day and night occupied in making penal laws, and in preparing and organizing instru-

ments and means of punishment. They build prisons, make chains and fetters, arrange places of exile and banishment, and different kinds of hardships and tortures, and think by these means to discipline criminals, whereas, in reality, they are causing destruction of morals and perversion of characters. The community, on the contrary, ought day and night to strive and endeavor with the utmost zeal and effort to accomplish the education of men, to cause them day by day to progress and to increase in science and knowledge, to acquire virtues, to gain good morals and to avoid vices, so that crimes may not occur. At the present time the contrary prevails; the community is always thinking of enforcing the penal laws, and of preparing means of punishment, instruments of death and chastisement, places for imprisonment and banishment; and they expect crimes to be committed. This has a demoralizing effect. But if the community would endeavor to educate the masses, day by day knowledge and sciences would increase, the understanding would be broadened, the sensibilities developed, customs would become good, and morals normal; in one word, in all these classes of perfections there would be progress, and there would be fewer crimes. It has been ascertained that among civilized peoples crime is less frequent than among uncivilized—that is to say, among those who have acquired the true civilization, which is divine civilization—the civilization of those who unite all the spiritual and material perfections. As ignorance is the cause of crimes, the more knowledge and science increases, the more crimes will diminish.[24]

See then how wide is the difference between material civilization and divine. With force and punishments, material civilization seeketh to restrain the people from mischief, from inflicting harm on society and committing crimes. But in a divine civilization, the individual is so conditioned that with no fear of punishment, he shunneth the perpetration of crimes, seeth the crime itself as the severest of torments, and with alacrity and joy, setteth himself to acquiring the virtues of humankind, to furthering human progress, and to spreading light across the world.[25]

Chapter Notes

1. *The Mind of Mahatma Gandhi.* Ed. R. K. Prabhu and U. R. Rao (Ahmedabad: Navajivan Publishing House, 1967), 112.

2. *The Mind of Mahatma Gandhi,* 147.

3. *Bahá'u'lláh,* A statement prepared by the Bahá'í International Community's Office of Public Information New York.

4. Shoghi Effendi, *God Passes By,* (Wilmette: Bahá'í Publishing Trust, 1987), 132–133.

5. 'Abdu'l-Bahá, quoted in *Kitáb-i-Aqdas* (Haifa: Bahá'í World Centre, 1992), 238–239.

6. J. E. Esslemont, *Bahá'u'lláh and the New Era* (Wilmette: Bahá'í Publishing Trust, 1976).

7. *The Mind of Mahatma Gandhi,* 416–417.

8. *The Mind of Mahatma Gandhi,* 417.

9. *The Mind of Mahatma Gandhi,* 416.

10. *All Men Are Brothers: Life and Thoughts of Mahatma Gandhi as Told in His Own Words.* Ed. K Kripalani (Paris: UNESCO, 1969), 118.

11. *Selections from the Writings of 'Abdu'l-Bahá* (Haifa: Bahá'í World Centre, 1978), 27–28.

12. *Selections from the Writings of 'Abdu'l-Bahá,* 289–290.

13. *The Mind of Mahatma Gandhi,* 115.

14. *The Mind of Mahatma Gandhi,* 115.

15. Bahá'u'lláh, quoted in *Bahá'u'lláh and the New Era,* 170–171.

16. *Selections from the Writings of 'Abdu'l-Bahá,* 197–198.

17. *Bahá'u'lláh and the New Era,* 170–171.

18. *The Mind of Mahatma Gandhi,* 147.

19. *The Mind of Mahatma Gandhi,* 137.

20. *The Mind of Mahatma Gandhi,* 135.

21. *The Promulgation of Universal Peace: Talks Delivered by 'Abdu'l-Bahá during His Visit to the United States and Canada in 1912* (Wilmette: Bahá'í Publishing Trust, 1982), 167.

22. *The Essential Writings of Mahatma Gandhi.* Ed. Raghavan Iyer (Oxford: Oxford University Press, 1990), 257–259.

23. *The Essential Writings of Mahatma Gandhi,* 264–265.

24. *Some Answered Questions.* (Wilmette: Bahá'í Publishing Trust, 1990), 268–272.

25. *Selections from the Writings of 'Abdu'l-Bahá,* 132–133.

Chapter 6

The Oneness of Humankind

The earth is but one country, and mankind its citizens.[1] All of us belong to humankind, but our society has yet to grasp the full meaning of this spiritual truth. Without understanding this principle, it is impossible to fathom or envision what is happening to society—what one great thinker called the "planetization" of humankind. As a result, humankind has yet a long way to go before we can finish the transition from the old world order, organized along the lines of "sovereign" and "independent" nations, to the new nonviolent civilization that is now only in its embryonic stage. Without the principle of the oneness of humankind, it is indeed difficult even to imagine a world ordered and governed globally through interdependent institutions of planetary scope. How can the earth become a common homeland if all of us are not fully and equally accepted as part of a single humanity? Indeed, it cannot!

The oneness of humankind is a lofty spiritual truth. Before contemplating its abstract, philosophical meaning and its higher implications, it might be instructive to look at it in more concrete terms through the scientific eyes of biology. We are a single biological species. According to a simplified rendering of contemporary biological thinking, when different communities of individuals of the same biological species stay isolated from each other for sufficiently long periods of time, biological *speciation* can occur.[2] This means that the distinct communities can no longer be considered a single species, for they lose the ability to interbreed viably and consistently. Humans, however, are very much a single biological species. People of every race, religion, and nationality can viably and consistently reproduce biologically with members of every other background. Indeed, today, we find that marriages between members of different ethnic and national backgrounds are steadily increasing. In fact, the offspring of such couples are potentially more healthy since there is less inbreeding and due to "hybrid vigor"—a biological term refering to the fact that genetically diverse offspring (hybrids) are more fit for survival (vigorous) than non-diverse organisms ("mutts are healthier than pure breeds"). Hence, the unity of humankind is a biological fact.

This fundamental truth was not clear in centuries past. In those times the peoples in different parts of the planet were to some extent isolated from each other. Such isolation allowed differences of race, language, and culture to grow and to self-perpetuate. Such ethnic and cultural diversity is not in itself sufficient to generate division and conflict. Nevertheless, when hatred and violence enter the picture, the results include disunity, racism, ethnocentrism, unbridled nationalism, religious bigotry, etc.—the stuff that fuels war. Hatred and violence directed towards those who are different from ourselves is the clearest sign that the principle of the oneness of humankind has not been understood and assimilated.

The principle of the oneness of humankind implies that all people are part of a single organism. In the Bahá'í view, recognition of the oneness of mankind "calls for no less than the reconstruction and the demilitarization of the whole civilized world—a world organically unified in all the essential aspects of its life, its political machinery, its spiritual aspiration, its trade and finance, its script and language, and yet infinite in the diversity of the national characteristics of its federated units."[3]

From a spiritual perspective, the concept of the oneness of humankind implies that our spiritual state is independent of our religious and cultural backgrounds. Differences of race, nationality etc. are less important to our spiritual condition than our spiritual qualities, such as our knowledge, our selflessness, and our zeal for

truth and compassion. Moreover, no human being—however ignorant and sick—should be considered "bad" or "evil," because all
of us are part of humankind. The spiritually sick must be nursed
back to spiritual health, through any means available, including
the wise application of as much force as may be necessary to ensure social order. Finally—and perhaps most controversially—the
oneness of humanity suggests that the humans alive today, those
who have already died, and those of the future are one and all
parts of a single, indivisible, living spiritual organism. People who
have died no longer have physical bodies, but in many cases the
ideas, actions, etc. that they have left for posterity continue to
bear fruit even today—evidence suggesting that the living and the
dead are not entirely separable.

The principle of the oneness of humankind is a central teaching of the Bahá'í Faith, and can also be found in the writings
of Gandhi. The following pages discuss their respective views in
greater detail.

6.1 The Origin of Oneness

Human minds can reflect on every subject matter, concrete and
abstract. Different minds can grasp the same truths, hence there
is something universal about the human mind. This is specifically
true in relation to the ability of the human mind to understand
the concept of the Oneness of God. According to both Gandhi and
the Bahá'ís, since God is One, therefore humanity must also be, on
a very fundamental level, a single undivided entity. 'Abdu'l-Bahá
writes:

> God is one; the effulgence of God is one; and humanity
> constitutes the servants of that one God. God is kind
> to all. He creates and provides for all; and all are under
> His care and protection. The Sun of Truth, the Word
> of God shines upon all mankind; the divine cloud pours
> down its precious rain; the gentle zephyrs of His mercy
> blow and all humanity is submerged in the ocean of His
> eternal justice and loving-kindness.[4]

All men are servants of the One God. One God reigns

over all the nations of the world and has pleasure in all
His children. All men are of one family; the crown of
humanity rests on the head of every human being.[5]

The following words of Gandhi show that he also saw the oneness
of humankind as a fundamental corollary of God's essential unity:

I believe in [the] absolute oneness of God and, therefore,
also of humanity. What though we have many bodies?
We have but one soul. The rays of the sun are many
through refraction. But they have the same source.
I cannot, therefore, detach myself from the wickedest
soul (nor may I be denied identity with the most virtuous). Whether, therefore, I will or not, I must involve
in my experiment the whole of my kind. Nor can I
do without experiment. Life is but an endless series of
experiments.[6]

6.2   One Organism

Several thousand years ago, the Greek philosopher Aristotle compared the body of humankind with the human body. Extending
the analogy, the various parts of society can be compared with the
different members and limbs of the human body. Our bodies are
made up of countless atoms and molecules that form cells, which
in turn form tissues and organs. These in turn are organized into
various systems—such as the digestive system, the nervous system,
etc.—that finally form one single entity: the human organism. But
this is not the highest level of organization. Far from it. Individual human beings constitute families and communities, which form
cities and nations. These in turn, are organized into continental
blocks, finally culminating in a single planetary human organism:
humankind.

As shown below, both Gandhi and the Bahá'ís have made use
of this analogy. An essential aspect of both the body of humankind
and the human body is that if one part suffers, every other part is
adversely affected.* The health of the whole reflects on the health

---

*See also Section 10.4.

of each component part, and vice-versa. Thus, if the liver becomes diseased, it can affect the kidneys and other organs. Similarly, if poverty—hence political instability—afflicts one nation, the rest of humanity will necessarily suffer the consequences. Concerning this theme, Bahá'u'lláh writes:

> O ye the elected representatives of the people in every land! Take ye counsel together, and let your concern be only for that which profiteth mankind, and bettereth the condition thereof, if ye be of them that scan heedfully. Regard the world as the human body which, though at its creation whole and perfect, hath been afflicted, through various causes, with grave disorders and maladies. Not for one day did it gain ease, nay its sickness waxed more severe, as it fell under the treatment of ignorant physicians, who gave full rein to their personal desires, and have erred grievously. And if, at one time, through the care of an able physician, a member of that body was healed, the rest remained afflicted as before. Thus informeth you the All-Knowing, the All-Wise.

> We behold it, in this day, at the mercy of rulers so drunk with pride that they cannot discern clearly their own best advantage, much less recognize a Revelation so bewildering and challenging as this. And whenever any one of them hath striven to improve its condition, his motive hath been his own gain, whether confessedly so or not; and the unworthiness of this motive hath limited his power to heal or cure.

> That which the Lord hath ordained as the sovereign remedy and mightiest instrument for the healing of all the world is the union of all its peoples in one universal Cause, one common Faith. This can in no wise be achieved except through the power of a skilled, an all-powerful and inspired Physician. This, verily, is the truth, and all else naught but error...[7]

Gandhi also viewed humankind as a single organism that cannot be adequately understood in reductionist terms, but only from

a "holistic" point of view. Commenting on the organic intercon-
nectedness of human life, he writes:

> ... the circulation of wealth in a nation resembles that
> of the blood in the natural body. There is one quick-
> ness of the current which comes of cheerful emotion or
> wholesome exercise; and another which comes of shame
> or fever. There is a flush of the body which is full of
> warmth and life; and another which will pass into pu-
> trefaction.[8]

> I claim that [the] human mind or human society is
> not divided into watertight compartments called so-
> cial, political, and religious. All act and react upon
> each other.[9]

> Human life being an undivided whole, no line can ever
> be drawn between its different compartments, nor be-
> tween ethics and politics.[9]

6.3   Unity in Diversity

In the human body, each organ, limb and member performs different tasks. There is division of labor: the heart pumps blood, the
lungs breathe air, the eyes and ears see and hear. Not all organs
can do the same thing, nor any single organ do everything. Each
part of the body has a specific set of capabilities and functions.
The organic oneness of the human body would not be possible if
every part were uniformly identical. Rather, the organic unity of
the human body emerges *because* of the great diversity of its constituent parts. If, like the human body, humankind is also a single
organism, then it follows that the same must be true of diversity
in human civilization. Diversity is thus an essential requirement in
order for unity to appear in humanity. If everyone was alike, the
wonderful division of labor that makes civilization possible would
disappear. Nobody can do everything, nor can everybody do the
same thing.

The need for diversity even has biological origins. For any organism to survive, its constituent parts must be diverse enough to

carry on a wide variety of very different tasks. Where there is a loss of diversity, weakness necessarily results. In plant species such as rice, for example, the most rugged and strong plants are "hybrids" that result from the interbreeding of different varieties. Although there are exceptions, the general rule is that inbreeding eventually leads to weak or malfunctioning individuals. Unfortunately, many people have not understood this simple truth. Hitler and the Nazis, for example, thought that they could engineer a "super" race of human beings by breeding human beings that are genetically uniform and "pure." Little did they realize that such uniformity, far from leading to a super-race, actually leads to inbreeding and loss of diversity in the human gene pool. Had such misinformed people known that diversity should be cultivated rather than destroyed, for example, they might have conceivably encouraged racial, religious, ideological and other kinds of diversity, instead of stamping it out. Alas, alas.

Diversity has also been stamped out in other, more subtle, ways. In many cultures, young men and women are discouraged, rather than encouraged, to marry outside their own race, nationality, caste, or religion. Similarly, people sometimes are prohibited from consorting, worshiping, or having fellowship with people of other backgrounds. Rather than appreciating the differences between us, they are taught to shun those who are different.

Prejudice can take many forms. Thus, racism leads to discriminatory treatment of people of another race. Excessive and unbridled nationalism can similarly cause harm to people of other nationalities. Religious intolerance is yet another example of a prejudice that can stifle diversity. As long as prejudices afflict humankind, it will not be fully able to appreciate the principle of the oneness of humankind, so racial, national, and religious prejudices will continue to undermine our collective efforts towards a truly nonviolent civilization. In the worst cases, violence and even death occur due to the perpetration of hate crimes motivated by attitudes of intolerance and extreme prejudice.

Over 20000 Bahá'ís were massacred in the first century of the Bahá'í Faith, and since the 1979 Islamic revolution in Iran, several hundred Bahá'ís have been executed, murdered, or gone missing. In Bahá'u'lláh's native land (at the time of writing of this book)

Bahá'ís still have their very basic rights denied to them on the basis of religion. The root cause of such problems is a lack of understanding of the fundamental principle of the oneness of humankind. Notwithstanding how they may be treated by others, and perhaps as a preemptive measure to help eradicate prejudices of every sort, Bahá'ís make a determined effort to consort with all peoples and the followers of all religions in a spirit of friendship and fellowship. In fact, Bahá'ís are commanded to do so by Bahá'u'lláh.[10]

Examples of prejudices addressed by Gandhi in his own country include the spectre of untouchability and caste-related discrimination.[11] Gandhi tried hard to integrate the untouchable community into the rest of society. Bahá'ís unhesitatingly agree that caste and all other prejudices should be abandoned.* After all, if humankind is a single organism, then rigid and hereditary caste divisions make little sense. Even worse, in practice such a system can easily lead to prejudice and disunity. In this light, it is interesting to note that while Gandhi was an uncompromising enemy of untouchability, he did accept, at least on a philosophical level, the ancient caste system of India.* He would, no doubt, have found it difficult to reject the caste system because it has Lord Krishna's explicit approval in the *Bhagavad Gita*, Gandhi's most cherished book.[12,13] Like Jawaharlal Nehru[14] and many other Indian contemporaries, Gandhi appears to have believed that the caste system was a good way—maybe the best way—of harmonizing the diverse elements of society into a unified and cohesive social organism. According to this view, the ancient Indians already had an understanding of the organic oneness of human society, so they applied this knowledge to achieve unity in diversity through the caste system. In Mahadev Desai's *The Gita According to Gandhi*, for example, we find the following description of the harmonizing aspects of the caste system:

> There was a system which existed in ages gone by, which served the then existing social organism magnificently, which was elastic and hence made it possible for a number of different groups of the same race and

---

*See also Section 13.7.

several races to live together in amity and peace. What we see today [the caste system] is its travesty, a fossil formed out of the incrustations of customs and practices of several centuries...

The division is no division into water-tight compartments... The division was entirely vocational, in order that each might serve the best interests of the organism. If men devoted themselves to tasks for which their character and aptitude best fitted them, they would be able to give of their best to the community.[15]

... division of the social organism is... based on what gifts and what special abilities one can bring to bear for the service of the organism.[16]

Bahá'ís believe that unity can only be achieved through the preservation—nay, cultivation—of diversity. However, they believe that the caste system is hopelessly outdated by several thousand years and incapable of solving contemporary social and economic problems, as should be expected according to the principle of progressive religious revelation.* We thus need a new system for managing diversity. The Bahá'ís have offered to the world—as a model for study—a new approach for achieving unity in diversity. By 1992, they already had in their worldwide religious community the representation of over 2100 nationalities and tribes.[17]

The fundamental principle that unity can only be achieved through diversity is a cornerstone of the Bahá'í Faith, as Shoghi Effendi eloquently explained in 1931:

Let there be no misgivings as to the animating purpose of the world-wide Law of Bahá'u'lláh. Far from aiming at the subversion of the existing foundations of society, it seeks to broaden its basis, to remold its institutions in a manner consonant with the needs of an ever-changing world. It can conflict with no legitimate allegiances, nor can it undermine essential loyalties. Its purpose is neither to stifle the flame of a

---

*See also Chapter 3

sane and intelligent patriotism in men's hearts, nor to
abolish the system of national autonomy so essential if
the evils of excessive centralization are to be avoided.
It does not ignore, nor does it attempt to suppress,
the diversity of ethnical origins, of climate, of history,
of language and tradition, of thought and habit, that
differentiate the peoples and nations of the world. It
calls for a wider loyalty, for a larger aspiration than
any that has animated the human race. It insists upon
the subordination of national impulses and interests to
the imperative claims of a unified world. It repudiates
excessive centralization on one hand, and disclaims all
attempts at uniformity on the other. Its watchword
is unity in diversity such as 'Abdu'l-Bahá Himself has
explained: "Consider the flowers of a garden. Though
differing in kind, color, form and shape, yet, inasmuch
as they are refreshed by the waters of one spring, re-
vived by the breath of one wind, invigorated by the
rays of one sun, this diversity increaseth their charm
and addeth unto their beauty. How unpleasing to the
eye if all the flowers and plants, the leaves and blos-
soms, the fruit, the branches and the trees of that garden were all of the same shape and color! Diversity of
hues, form and shape enricheth and adorneth the garden, and heighteneth the effect thereof. In like manner,
when divers shades of thought, temperament and character, are brought together under the power and influence of one central agency, the beauty and glory of
human perfection will be revealed and made manifest.
Naught but the celestial potency of the Word of God,
which ruleth and transcendeth the realities of all things,
is capable of harmonizing the divergent thoughts, sentiments, ideas and convictions of the children of men."
The call of Bahá'u'lláh is primarily directed against
all forms of provincialism, all insularities and prejudices. If long-cherished ideals and time-honored institutions, if certain social assumptions and religious for-
mulae have ceased to promote the welfare of the gener-

ality of mankind, if they no longer minister to the needs
of a continually evolving humanity, let them be swept
away and relegated to the limbo of obsolescent and for-
gotten doctrines. Why should these, in a world subject
to the immutable law of change and decay, be exempt
from the deterioration that must needs overtake every
human institution? For legal standards, political and
economic theories are solely designed to safeguard the
interests of humanity as a whole, and not humanity to
be crucified for the preservation of the integrity of any
particular law or doctrine.[18]

It may interest the reader to note the similarities in the following statements belonging to Bahá'u'lláh and to Gandhi respectively:

Ye are all the leaves of one tree and the drops of one
ocean.[19]

We are all leaves of a majestic tree whose trunk cannot be shaken off its roots which are deep down in the
bowels of the earth.[20]

Chapter Notes

1. This is one of the most celebrated statements of Bahá'u'lláh, and can be found in a number of his works. See, for example, *Gleanings from the Writings of Bahá'u'lláh*. Trans. Shoghi Effendi (Wilmette: Bahá'í Publishing Trust, 1976), 250.

2. The reader should note that the word "species" is used here in its technical biological meaning, and not in any other. The word also appears in provisional English translations of some original Bahá'í documents in Persian, where the intended meaning is possibly very different from the biological one. These texts were not translated into English by Shoghi Effendi, the Guardian of the Bahá'í Faith, so it is conceivable that future translations may use a word other than "species" to clear the ambiguity. The following comment, taken from *Bahá'u'lláh and the New Era*, clearly supports the view that this word has two very different meanings: *The word "species" is used here to explain the distinction which has always existed between men and animals, despite outward appearances. It should not be read with its current specialized biological meaning.* See J. E. Esslemont, *Bahá'u'lláh and the New Era*, 5th rev. ed. (Wilmette: Bahá'í Publishing Trust, 1987), 206.

3. *The Promise of World Peace.* A statement of the Universal House of Justice addressed to the peoples of the world, dated October 1985.

4. *Foundations of World Unity* (Wilmette: Bahá'í Publishing Trust, 1979), 92.

5. *Paris Talks: Addresses given by 'Abdu'l-Bahá in Paris in 1911–1912* (London: Bahá'í Publishing Trust, 1972), 138–40.

6. *The Mind of Mahatma Gandhi.* Ed. R. K. Prabhu and U. R. Rao (Ahmedabad: Navajivan Publishing House, 1967), 8.

7. *The Proclamation of Bahá'u'lláh* (Wilmette: Bahá'í Publishing Trust, 1978), 67–68

8. *The Selected Works of Mahatma Gandhi: Volume Four (the Basic Works).* Ed. Shriman Narayan (Ahmedabad: Navajivan Publishing House, 1968), 59–60.

9. *The Mind of Mahatma Gandhi,* 101.

10. *Kitáb-i-Aqdas* (Haifa: Bahá'í World Centre, 1992).

11. The word untouchable refers to people who were considered ritually unclean and who typically cleaned the human waste in "latrines."

Gandhi believed that the practice of untouchability was a "blot on Hinduism" (Young India, April 27, 1921) and that it had no genuine religious basis. He renamed them *harijans* (born of God) and worked hard to integrate them into the rest of society.

12. *The Gospel of Selfless Action or The Gita According to Gandhi.* Ed. Mahadev Desai (Ahmedabad: Navajivan Publishing House, 1984).

13. Gandhi's translation of the *Gita* shows that he was not against the caste system in principle. Rather, he upheld its philosophical and religious basis. There are numerous instances of his giving moral support to the caste system, e.g. his views on intermarriage, etc.

14. Jawaharlal Nehru. *Discovery of India* (London: Meridian Books, 1960).

15. *The Gospel of Selfless Action or The Gita According to Gandhi,* 102–3.

16. *The Gospel of Selfless Action or The Gita According to Gandhi,* 99.

17. *Bahá'u'lláh,* A statement prepared by the Bahá'í International Community's Office of Public Information New York.

18. Shoghi Effendi, *The World Order of Bahá'u'lláh.* (Wilmette: Bahá'í Publishing Trust, 1991), 41–2.

19. *Tablets of Bahá'u'lláh Revealed after the Kitáb-i-Aqdas* (Wilmette: Bahá'í Publishing Trust, 1988), 129.

20. *The Essential Writings of Mahatma Gandhi,* 348.

Chapter 7

Balancing the Sexes

A nonviolent civilization can flourish only when the different parts of society are at peace with each other. There has been tremendous progress with respect to the rights and privileges enjoyed by women in many countries. However, men continue to dominate women in politics and many other areas. This imbalance hurts not only women but also the men, according to the principle of the oneness of humankind.* This chapter examines what Gandhi and the Bahá'ís have to say about gender relations.

7.1 Spiritual Equality

Common to both the world view of Gandhi and the Bahá'í teachings is the shared belief that women and men are spiritually and mentally equal. There is no difference between the "souls" of men and women, so they deserve equal treatment and privileges. Writing about the equality of the sexes, Gandhi explains:

> Woman is the companion of man gifted with equal mental capacities. She has the right to participate in the minutest detail of the activities of man, and she has the same right of freedom and liberty as he.[1]

The same idea is found in the writings of 'Abdu'l-Bahá:

---

*See also Chapter 6.

Equality of the sexes will be established in proportion
to the increased opportunities afforded woman in this
age, for man and woman are equally the recipients of
powers and endowments from God, the Creator. God
has not ordained distinction between them in His con-
summate purpose.[2]

Indeed, 'Abdu'l-Bahá writes of a glorious future for women:

In the Dispensation of Bahá'u'lláh, women are advanc-
ing side by side with men. There is no area or instance
where they will lag behind: they have equal rights with
men, and will enter, in the future, into all branches of
the administration of society. Such will be their eleva-
tion that, in every area of endeavour, they will occupy
the highest levels in the human world. Rest thou assured. Look not upon their present state. In future,
the world of womankind will shine with lustrous bril-
liance, for such is the will and purpose of Bahá'u'lláh.
At the time of elections the right to vote is the inalienable right of women, and the entrance of women into
all human departments is an irrefutable and incontrovertible question. No soul can retard or prevent it.[3]

Gandhi explains that the essential equality of men and women
does not mean they are in every way identical:

Nevertheless there is no doubt that at some point there
is bifurcation. Whilst both are fundamentally one, it is
equally true that in the form there is a vital difference
between the two. Hence the vocations of the two must
also be different. The duty of motherhood, which the
vast majority of women will always undertake, requires
qualities which the man need not possess.[4]

How can women and men, who are different from each other on
many levels, be said to be equal? The answer is simple. They are
equal because through their differences women and men complement each other, and neither can live without the other. Indeed,
without the cooperation of men and women, the human species
would become extinct—literally. Gandhi writes,

My own opinion is that, just as fundamentally man and
woman are one, their problem must be one in essence.
The soul in both is the same. The two live the same
life, have the same feelings. Each is the complement
of the other. The one cannot live without the other's
active help.[5]

'Abdu'l-Bahá explains this same concept using a simple but powerful metaphor:

And among the teachings of Bahá'u'lláh is the equality of women and men. The world of humanity has
two wings – one is women and the other men. Not until both wings are equally developed can the bird fly.
Should one wing remain weak, flight is impossible. Not
until the world of women becomes equal to the world
of men in the acquisition of virtues and perfections,
can success and prosperity be attained as they ought
to be.[6]

He extends this idea further:

The world of humanity consists of two parts: male and
female. Each is the complement of the other. Therefore, if one is defective, the other will necessarily be
incomplete, and perfection cannot be attained. There
is a right hand and a left hand in the human body, func-
tionally equal in service and administration. If either
proves defective, the defect will naturally extend to the
other by involving the completeness of the whole; for
accomplishment is not normal unless both are perfect.
If we say one hand is deficient, we prove the inability
and incapacity of the other; for single-handed there is
no full accomplishment. Just as physical accomplishment is complete with two hands, so man and woman,
the two parts of the social body, must be perfect. It is
not natural that either should remain undeveloped; and
until both are perfected, the happiness of the human
world will not be realized.[7]

It follows naturally that men will fail to achieve their full potential until women are given equal opportunities to advance. 'Abdu'l-Bahá writes,

> Women have equal rights with men upon earth; in religion and society they are a very important element. As long as women are prevented from attaining their highest possibilities, so long will men be unable to achieve the greatness which might be theirs.[8]

7.2   Sexism: Roots and Remedies

The question may be asked of how men came to dominate women, given that men and women are equal. Gandhi believed that men's dominance over women is perpetuated primarily through a lack of proper education and the false—extremely harmful—teaching that men are superior to women: He writes,

> But somehow or other man has dominated woman from ages past, and so woman has developed an inferiority complex. She has believed in the truth of man's interested teaching that she is inferior to him. But the seers among men have recognized their equal status.[9]

'Abdu'l-Bahá similarly cites lack of education as the primary reason for the inequality of men and women.

> Woman's lack of progress and proficiency has been due to her need of equal education and opportunity. Had she been allowed this equality, there is no doubt she would be the counterpart of man in ability and capacity. The happiness of mankind will be realized when women and men coordinate and advance equally, for each is the complement and helpmeet of the other.[10]

Although in the past men have dominated over women, 'Abdu'l-Bahá explains that this dominance relationship is fast giving way to a more healthy and equal relationship between men and women:

> The world in the past has been ruled by force, and man has dominated over woman by reason of his more forceful and aggressive qualities both of body and mind. But

the balance is already shifting; force is losing its dominance, and mental alertness, intuition, and the spiritual qualities of love and service, in which woman is strong, are gaining ascendancy. Hence the new age will be an age less masculine and more permeated with the feminine ideals, or, to speak more exactly, will be an age in which the masculine and feminine elements of civilization will be more evenly balanced.[11]

Having noted that the inequality of men and women is unjust and unhealthy, we can ask how people can foster the emancipation and progress of women, hence the advancement of humankind as a whole. Both Gandhi and the Bahá'ís agree that the roots of the problem lie in the lack of proper education. Bahá'ís thus give great importance to the education of girls, because as mothers they are potentially the first educators of their future children. 'Abdu'l-Bahá writes,

... those present should concern themselves with every means of training the girl children; with teaching the various branches of knowledge, good behaviour, a proper way of life, the cultivation of a good character, chastity and constancy, perseverance, strength, determination, firmness of purpose; with household management, the education of children, and whatever especially applieth to the needs of girls—to the end that these girls, reared in the stronghold of all perfections, and with the protection of a goodly character, will, when they themselves become mothers, bring up their children from earliest infancy to have a good character and conduct themselves well.[12]

Not surprisingly, Bahá'ís give preference to the education of girls over boys. 'Abdu'l-Bahá writes,

Furthermore, the education of woman is more necessary and important than that of man, for woman is the trainer of the child from its infancy. If she be defective and imperfect herself, the child will necessarily be deficient; therefore, imperfection of woman implies a condition of imperfection in all mankind, for it is the mother who rears, nurtures and guides the growth of the child. This is not the function of the father. If the educator be incompetent, the educated will be correspondingly lacking. This is evident and incontrovertible. Could the student be brilliant and accomplished if the teacher is illiterate and ignorant? The mothers are the first educators of mankind; if they be imperfect, alas for the condition and future of the race.[13]

Other ways to help women (and hence humankind) to advance may be inferred from some of Gandhi's writings. He condemned the physical and mental abuse of women by men. Such abuse includes but is not limited to domestic violence, rape, verbal abuse, and war. Gandhi writes,

Of all the evils for which man has made himself responsible, none is so degrading, so shocking or so brutal as his abuse of the better half of humanity—to me, the female sex, not the weaker sex. It is the nobler of the two, for it is even today the embodiment of sacrifice, silent suffering, humility, faith and knowledge.[14]

Ironically, the oppression and abuse of women can be both astonishingly subtle and harsh concurrently. For on the one hand women are often given fewer privileges than men in important respects, but on the other hand more is frequently demanded from women. One example of this double standard is the ethics of sex. Women are often pressured on multiple fronts to become sexual objects, but at the same time they are expected to be more faithful and "pure" than their often unfaithful male counterparts. Gandhi disliked such hypocritical obsession with "female purity," and felt that this double standard was unhealthy:[15]

And why is there all this morbid anxiety about female purity? Have women any say in the matter of male purity? We hear nothing of women's anxiety about men's chastity. Why should men arrogate to themselves the right to regulate female purity? It cannot be superimposed from without. It is a matter of evolution from within and therefore of self-effort.[16]

7.3 Women and World Peace

Can the emancipation of women be related to the establishment
of international peace? The idea may sound radical to many, but
Bahá'ís hold the view, shared by Gandhi, that the emancipation
of women is directly related to the ushering in of world peace and
to the prosperity of humankind. Speaking about the teachings of
Bahá'u'lláh in 1912, 'Abdu'l-Bahá said,

> He [Bahá'u'lláh] promulgated the adoption of the same
> course of education for man and woman. Daugh-
> ters and sons must follow the same curriculum of
> study, thereby promoting unity of the sexes. When
> all mankind shall receive the same opportunity of edu-
> cation and the equality of men and women be realized,
> the foundations of war will be utterly destroyed...[17]

Gandhi echoed this theme a few decades later when he wrote
rhetorically,

> If only women would forget that they belong to the
> weaker sex, I have no doubt that they can do infinitely
> more than men against war. Answer for yourselves
> what your great soldiers and generals would do, if their
> wives and daughters and mothers refused to counte-
> nance their participation in militarism in any shape or
> form.[18]

'Abdu'l-Bahá gave a clear picture of how women can help bring
international peace.

> ... the principle of religion has been revealed by
> Bahá'u'lláh that woman must be given the privilege of
> equal education with man and full right to his preroga-
> tives. That is to say, there must be no difference in the
> education of male and female in order that womankind
> may develop equal capacity and importance with man
> in the social and economic equation. Then the world
> will attain unity and harmony. In past ages human-
> ity has been defective and inefficient because it has
> been incomplete. War and its ravages have blighted

the world; the education of woman will be a mighty
step toward its abolition and ending, for she will use
her whole influence against war. Woman rears the child
and educates the youth to maturity. She will refuse to
give her sons for sacrifice upon the field of battle. In
truth, she will be the greatest factor in establishing universal peace and international arbitration. Assuredly,
woman will abolish warfare among mankind...[19]

Moreover, in answer to a seeker who asked about the prerequisites
for world peace, 'Abdu'l-Bahá said,

[A] fact of [great] importance in bringing about international peace is woman's suffrage. That is to say,
when perfect equality shall be established between men
and women, peace may be realized for the simple reason that womankind in general will never favor warfare. Women will not be willing to allow those whom
they have so tenderly cared for to go to the battlefield.
When they shall have a vote, they will oppose any cause
of warfare. Another factor which will bring about universal peace is the linking together of the Orient and
the Occident.[20]

This link between the emancipation of women and world peace
is considered sufficiently important by the Bahá'ís that, as late as
in 1985, the Universal House of Justice* wrote the following in a
letter addressed to the peoples of the world, titled *The Promise of
World Peace:*

The emancipation of women, the achievement of full
equality between the sexes, is one of the most important, though less acknowledged prerequisites of peace.
The denial of such equality perpetrates an injustice
against one half of the world's population and promotes in men harmful attitudes and habits that are
carried from the family to the workplace, to political
life, and ultimately to international relations. There

---

*The supreme ruling body of the Bahá'í Faith. See chapter 1.

are no grounds, moral, practical, or biological, upon which such denial can be justified. Only as women are welcomed into full partnership in all fields of human endeavour will the moral and psychological climate be created in which international peace can emerge.[21]

7.4 A Balanced Age

Equality of the sexes requires that both halves of the population achieve their fullest potential. Specifically, (i) women need to be provided an education which is equal to that of men so that they can develop qualities and skills traditionally only possessed by men; and (ii) men must learn to value and acquire attributes traditionally considered "feminine," such as compassion, patience, etc.

Physical strength, aggression, and violence, which men excel at, have in the past been highly valued. But the belief that aggression, force, and violence are the essential indicators of real strength is inconsistent with faith in the power of a merciful and compassionate God who advises us to "turn the other cheek." As humankind slowly realizes the almost limitless power of non-violence and compassion, such materialistic and primitive ideas about physical force and aggression will yield to an appreciation of nonviolent, spiritual strength—a new kind of courage with subtly "feminine" overtones. It may interest the reader to know that 'Abdu'l-Bahá said,

> The woman has greater moral courage than the man...[22]

And Gandhi said,

> If they would realize the strength of non-violence they would not consent to be called the weaker sex.[23]

Chapter Notes

1. *All Men Are Brothers: Life and Thoughts of Mahatma Gandhi as Told in His Own Words*. Ed. K Kripalani (Paris: UNESCO, 1969), 162.

2. *The Promulgation of Universal Peace: Talks Delivered by 'Abdu'l-Bahá during His Visit to the United States and Canada in 1912* (Wilmette: Bahá'í Publishing Trust, 1982), 300.

3. *Paris Talks: Addresses given by 'Abdu'l-Bahá in Paris in 1911–1912* (London: Bahá'í Publishing Trust, 1972), 182.

4. *All Men Are Brothers*, 162.

5. *All Men Are Brothers*, 160.

6. *Selections from the Writings of 'Abdu'l-Bahá* (Haifa: Baha i World Centre, 1978), 302.

7. *The Promulgation of Universal Peace*, 134.

8. *Paris Talks*, 133.

9. *All Men Are Brothers*, 160.

10. *The Promulgation of Universal Peace*, 182.

11. 'Abdu'l-Bahá, quoted in J. E. Esslemont, *Bahá'u'lláh and the New Era*, 5th rev. ed. (Wilmette: Bahá'í Publishing Trust, 1987), 149.

12. *Selections from the Writings of 'Abdu'l-Bahá*, 123–24.

13. See *The Promulgation of Universal Peace*, 133–137.

14. *All Men Are Brothers*, 161.

15. Gandhi found in his personal life that it was through according greater rights to his wife that he was able to earn his wife's heartfelt respect. He tried to practice what he preached about equality, and had little patience for sexual hypocrisy: "If I were born a woman, I would rise in rebellion against any pretension on the part of man that woman is born to be his plaything. I have mentally become a woman in order to steal into her heart. I could not steal into my wife's heart until I decided to treat her differently than I used to do, and so I restored to her all her rights by dispossessing myself of all my so-called rights as her husband." See *All Men Are Brothers*, 161.

16. *All Men Are Brothers*, 161.

17. See *The Promulgation of Universal Peace*, 174–175.

18. *All Men Are Brothers*, 163.

19. See *The Promulgation of Universal Peace*, 108.

20. See *The Promulgation of Universal Peace*, 167.

21. *The Promise of World Peace*. A statement of the Universal House of Justice addressed to the peoples of the world, dated October 1985.

22. *'Abdu'l-Bahá in London: Addresses, and Notes of Conversations* (London: Bahá'í Publishing Trust, 1982), 102–103.

23. *All Men Are Brothers*, 162.

Chapter 8

Education

At birth, a human being—a baby—knows almost nothing. When we come out of the womb into the real world, we practically know only how to cry, breathe and suckle at the breast. Hence, the learning process starts at birth, if not before. Then we become children. We learn not only from our teachers during our years at school, but also from our parents and grandparents—indeed also from friends, enemies, animals, experiences, etc. Even after we "grow up," the learning process never stops at school or college, but rather continues until death or senility. Education is thus one of the most important life-long aspects of the human experience. Yet, judging by the literacy rates around the world near the beginning of the third millennium,* it is probably fair to say that our present civilization has miserably failed to educate our brothers and sisters of the world—even just to read and write. From the perspective of the educational process, there is something fundamentally wrong with our parenting, our educational institutions and our communities at large. Fortunately, in recent years there have been remarkable changes aimed at remedying the deplorable situation. Rather than blindly imitating those who came before us, more and more people are beginning to think independently about the importance of good education. An excellent development is how even extremely poor people everywhere are slowly beginning to demand, to the

---

*Of the Common Era.

extent possible, basic education for their children. More people
are beginning to value education. This chapter briefly examines
the subject of education as explored in the writings of Gandhi and
of the Bahá'í Faith.

8.1   What is it?

Is education merely the progressive refinement and training of the
human intellect? Or does human education necessarily involve the
development of human faculties besides the intellect? A concept
found in both Gandhi's writings and the Bahá'í sacred texts is that
education is a progressive and ongoing process of human transformation. Education leads the individual from the condition of the
animal at birth to that of a thinking, intelligent, compassionate
human being—and eventually even beyond: towards the divine.
One of Bahá'u'lláh's best known metaphors is the analogy comparing the human mind to a mirror or gem that requires polishing
before it can reflect the light of God's divine attributes.[1] Education, according to this view, is the progressive "polishing" of the
mirror of the human heart. The goal of education is to transmute
the human animal into a spiritual being, whose heart shines like a
"gem of divine virtue".[2] Bahá'u'lláh explains further:

> Man is the supreme Talisman. Lack of a proper edu-
> cation hath, however, deprived him of that which he
> doth inherently possess... The Great Being saith: Re-
> gard man as a mine rich in gems of inestimable value.
> Education can, alone, cause it to reveal its treasures,
> and enable mankind to benefit therefrom...[3]

Education as referred to here is not identical to book learning.
Esslemont explains:

> At present a really well educated man is the rarest of
> phenomena, for nearly everyone has false prejudices,
> wrong ideals, erroneous conceptions and bad habits
> drilled into him from babyhood. How few are taught
> from their earliest childhood to love God with all their
> hearts and dedicate their lives to Him; to regard service

to humanity as the highest aim in life; to develop their powers to the best advantage for the general good of all! Yet surely these are the essential elements of a good education. Mere cramming of the memory with facts about arithmetic, grammar, geography, languages, etc., has comparatively little effect in producing noble and useful lives.[4]

Similarly, Gandhi held the view that education is not the mere training of the intellect, but rather that it is a process with the potential to transform our very essence, by helping to bring out in the individual the finest attributes of humanity:

> Real education consists in drawing the best out of yourself.[5]

> By education I mean an all-round drawing out of the best in child and man—body, mind, and spirit.[6]

8.2 Education and Service

Explaining the relationship between freedom and education, Gandhi suggests that the criterion for judging the worth of education is its potential for serving humanity. He defines education as follows:

> The ancient aphorism, 'Education is that which liberates' is as true today as it was before. Education here does not mean mere spiritual knowledge, nor does liberation signify only spiritual liberation after death. Knowledge includes all training that is useful for the service of mankind and liberation means freedom from all manner of servitude even in the present life. Servitude is of two kinds: slavery to domination from outside and to one's own artificial needs. The knowledge acquired in the pursuit of this ideal alone constitutes true study.[7]

The idea that education is a means to a higher End, namely worship of God through service to humanity, is also found explic-

itly in the Bahá'í writings.   We read in the notes to the Kitáb-i-
Aqdas (the Most Holy Book), that Bahá'u'lláh *counsels people to
study such sciences and arts as are "useful" and would further "the
progress and advancement" of society.*[8] Furthermore, Bahá'u'lláh
writes:

> Knowledge is as wings to man's life, and a ladder for
> his ascent. Its acquisition is incumbent upon everyone.
> The knowledge of such sciences, however, should be
> acquired as can profit the peoples of the earth...[9]

While Gandhi genuinely felt that education is "that which lib-
erates," he did not undervalue the knowledge of the sciences taught
traditionally, for he writes,

> I value education in the different sciences. Our children
> cannot have too much of chemistry and physics.[10]

It is of interest to note that Gandhi's definition of education
quoted above alludes to the ironic idea that true liberty consists in
becoming a servant of humanity. 'Abdu'l-Bahá, who underwent 40
years of exile and imprisonment, declared during a visit to London:
"There is no prison but the prison self..."[11] Accordingly, a primary
goal of education should be to help liberate us from mental slavery
to outside pressures and from inner personal limitations, so that
we may become free to worship God through unfettered service to
humanity. 'Abdu'l-Bahá explains:

> Freedom is not a matter of place. It is a condition. I
> was thankful for the prison, and the lack of liberty was
> very pleasing to me, for those days were passed in the
> path of service, under the utmost difficulties and trials,
> bearing fruits and results.

> Unless one accepts dire vicissitudes, he will not attain.
> To me prison is freedom, troubles rest me, death is life,
> and to be despised is honour. Therefore, I was happy
> all that time in prison. When one is released from the
> prison of self, that is indeed release, for that is the
> greater prison. When this release takes place, then one
> cannot be outwardly imprisoned. When they put my

feet in stocks, I would say to the guard, 'You cannot imprison me, for here I have light and air and bread and water. There will come a time when my body will be in the ground, and I shall have neither light nor air nor food nor water, but even then I shall not be imprisoned.' The afflictions which come to humanity sometimes tend to centre the consciousness upon the limitations, and this is a veritable prison. Release comes by making of the will a Door through which the confirmations of the Spirit come.[11]

8.3 Moral education

The belief that the ultimate goal of education is the service of humankind has an important logical consequence: a heightened awareness of the need to give priority to education in morals and ethics. 'Abdu'l-Bahá writes:

> Training in morals and good conduct is far more important than book learning. A child that is cleanly, agreeable, of good character, well-behaved—even though he be ignorant—is preferable to a child that is rude, unwashed, ill-natured, and yet becoming deeply versed in all the sciences and arts. The reason for this is that the child who conducts himself well, even though he be ignorant, is of benefit to others, while an ill-natured, ill-behaved child is corrupted and harmful to others, even though he be learned. If, however, the child be trained to be both learned and good, the result is light upon light.[12]

Writing to Bahá'í educators of ·his time, 'Abdu'l-Bahá explained,

> It is certain that ye will... draw up plans for the opening of a number of schools. These schools for academic studies must at the same time be training centres in behaviour and conduct, and they must favour character and conduct above the sciences and arts. Good be-

haviour and high moral character must come first, for
unless the character be trained, acquiring knowledge
will only prove injurious. Knowledge is praiseworthy
when it is coupled with ethical conduct and virtuous
character; otherwise it is a deadly poison, a frightful
danger. A physician of evil character, and who be-
trayeth his trust, can bring on death, and become the
source of numerous infirmities and diseases.[13]

Gandhi also realized the need for moral education, and accorded
it the highest priority:

Religious, that is ethical, education will occupy first
place.[14]

Literary training by itself adds not one inch to one's
moral height and character-building is independent of
literary training.[15]

I would develop in the child his hands, his brain and
his soul. The hands have almost atrophied. The soul
has been altogether ignored.[16]

Gandhi, moreover, held a holistic concept of education, and felt
that moral education cannot be artificially separated from physical
and intellectual training:

I hold that true education of the intellect can only come
through a proper exercise and training of the bodily organs, e.g., hands, feet, eyes, ears, nose, etc. In other
words an intelligent use of the bodily organs in a child
provides the best and quickest way of developing his
intellect. But unless the development of the mind and
body goes hand in hand with a corresponding awakening of the soul, the former alone would prove to be
a poor lopsided affair. By spiritual training I mean
education of the heart. A proper and all-round development of the mind, therefore, can take place only
when it proceeds *pari passu* with the education of the
physical and spiritual faculties of the child. They constitute an indivisible whole. According to this theory,

therefore, it would be a gross fallacy to suppose that they can be developed piecemeal or independently of one another.[17]

8.4 Musical Education

Both Gandhi and the Bahá'ís give importance to musical training. Gandhi writes:

> ... music should form part of the syllabus of primary education... The modulation of the voice is as necessary as the training of the hand. Physical drill, handicrafts, drawing, and music should go hand in hand in order to draw the best out of boys and girls and create in them a real interest in tuition.[18]

Relating musical instruction to the potentially uplifting and positive effects of music on our emotions, 'Abdu'l-Bahá writes:

> The art of music is divine and effective. It is the food of the soul and spirit. Through the power and charm of music the spirit of man is uplifted. It has wonderful sway and effect in the hearts of children, for their hearts are pure and melodies have great influence in them. The latent talents with which the hearts of these children are endowed will find expression through the medium of music. Therefore, you must exert yourselves to make them proficient; teach them to sing with excellence and effect. It is incumbent upon each child to know something of music, for without knowledge of this art the melodies of instrument and voice cannot be rightly enjoyed. Likewise, it is necessary that the schools teach it in order that the souls and hearts of the pupils may become vivified and exhilarated and their lives be brightened with enjoyment.[19]

It may interest the reader to note that music has been shown to be related to human neurophysiology, and might even be potentially important for health.

8.5   Sex Education

Human sexuality is one of the subjects in which Gandhi and the
Bahá'ís have important differences of opinion.* Nevertheless, they
do agree that besides teaching basic knowledge about maintaining
proper hygiene and health, it is very important to teach children
about reproduction and sex. Sex and reproduction, though related,
are far from being the same thing.

Sex education presents a challenge because on the one hand,
great care must be taken to protect children from the extremely
harmful effects of dangerous puritanical philosophies that tend to
demonize human sexuality. On the other hand, it also becomes
vital to teach children, from a young age, the value and necessity of leading a chaste and holy life. Such values are especially
vital in these days of sexual permissiveness and instant gratifi-
cation. The knowledge of how to regulate and channel—but not
repress—sexual desires and how to restrain the violent, animalistic
side of human sexuality may very well help to avoid the evils of pae-
dophilia, rape, and the other numerous, unacceptable, distorted,
expressions of sexuality that currently plague society.

Relating basic sex education with training in self-restraint,
Gandhi writes,

> We cannot properly control or conquer the sexual pas-
> sion by turning a blind eye to it. I am, therefore,
> strongly in favour of teaching young boys and young
> girls the significance and right use of their generative
> organs. In my own way I have tried to impart this
> knowledge to young children of both sexes, for whose
> training I was responsible. But the sex education that
> I stand for must have for its object the conquest and
> sublimation of the sex passion. Such education should
> automatically serve to bring home to children the es-
> sential distinction between man and brute, to make
> them realize that it is man's privilege and pride to be
> gifted with the faculties of head and heart both, that
> he is a thinking no less than a feeling animal, and to re-

---

*See also Section 13.4.

nounce the sovereignty of reason over the blind instinct is, therefore, to renounce man's estate. In man, reason quickens and guides the feeling, in brute the soul lies ever dormant. To awaken the heart is to awaken the dormant soul, to awaken reason and to inculcate discrimination between good and evil. Today, our entire environment—our reading, our thinking, and our social behaviour—is generally calculated to subserve and cater for the sex urge. To break through its coils is no easy task. But it is a task worthy of our highest endeavour.[20]

'Abdu'l-Bahá also emphasized the need to teach honor, holiness and chastity to children while they are still young:

Children are even as a branch that is fresh and green; they will grow up in whatever way you train them. Take the utmost care to give them high ideals and goals, so that once they come of age, they will cast their beams like brilliant candles on the world, and will not be defiled by lusts and passions in the way of animals, heedless and unaware, but instead will set their hearts on achieving everlasting honour and acquiring all the excellences of humankind.[21]

8.6 Discipline

Educating a child requires a delicate balance between love and encouragement on the one hand, and gentle disciplinary measures on the other. But abuse is absolutely forbidden, as 'Abdu'l-Bahá explains:

It is not... permissible to strike a child, or vilify him, for the child's character will be totally perverted if he be subjected to blows or verbal abuse.[22]

Indeed, according to Gandhi sometimes it is better to allow children to learn on their own:

A wise parent allows the children to make mistakes. It is good for them once in a while to burn their fingers.[23]

8.7   Universal Education

The cause of universal education for every human child was one
of Gandhi's cherished ideals. He was especially concerned with
the education of the poor. For example, he diligently tried in the
1940's to educate difficult-to-reach village children in India to turn
them into model villagers.[24]

Bahá'ís share this desire to educate every human child. In
the Kitáb-i-Aqdas, Bahá'u'lláh makes it compulsory to educate
children.[25] More recently in 1985, the Universal House of Justice*
wrote in *The Promise of World Peace*:

> The cause of universal education, which has already
> enlisted in its service an army of dedicated people from
> every faith and nation, deserves the utmost support
> that the governments of the world can lend it. For
> ignorance is indisputably the principal reason for the
> decline and fall of peoples and the perpetuation of prej-
> udice. No nation can achieve success unless education
> is accorded all its citizens. Lack of resources limits
> the ability of many nations to fulfil this necessity, im-
> posing a certain ordering of priorities. The decision-
> making agencies involved would do well to consider giv-
> ing first priority to the education of women and girls,
> since it is through educated mothers that the benefits
> of knowledge can be most effectively and rapidly dif-
> fused throughout society. In keeping with the require-
> ments of the times, consideration should also be given
> to teaching the concept of world citizenship as part of
> the standard education of every child.[26]

---

*The supreme ruling body of the Bahá'í international community. See
Chapter 1.

Chapter Notes

1. See *The Hidden Words of Bahá'u'lláh* (Wilmette: Bahá'í Publishing Trust, 1985). See also *Kitáb-i-Íqán* (Wilmette: Bahá'í Publishing Trust, 1989), 68–9, and also *Gleanings from the Writings of Bahá'u'lláh.* (Wilmette: Bahá'í Publishing Trust, 1976), 261–4. Trans. Shoghi Effendi.

2. *Hidden Words*, 3.

3. *Gleanings,* 259–60.

4. J. E. Esslemont, *Bahá'u'lláh and the New Era,* 5th rev. ed. (Wilmette: Bahá'í Publishing Trust, 1987), 151.

5. *All Men Are Brothers: Life and Thoughts of Mahatma Gandhi as Told in His Own Words.* Ed. K Kripalani (Paris: UNESCO, 1969), 151.

6. *All Men Are Brothers,* 151.

7. *The Mind of Mahatma Gandhi.* Ed. R. K. Prabhu and U. R. Rao (Ahmedabad: Navajivan Publishing House, 1967), 377.

8. *Kitáb-i-Aqdas* (Haifa: Bahá'í World Centre, 1992), 192.

9. *Tablets of Bahá'u'lláh Revealed after the Kitáb-i-Aqdas* (Wilmette: Bahá'í Publishing Trust, 1988), 51–52.

10. *All Men Are Brothers,* 158.

11. *'Abdu'l-Bahá in London: Addresses, and Notes of Conversations.* (London: Bahá'í Publishing Trust, 1982), 120–1.

12. *Selections from the Writings of 'Abdu'l-Bahá.* (Haifa: Bahá'í World Centre, 1978), 135–36

13. *A Compilation on Bahá'í Education Compiled by the Research Department of the Universal House of Justice* (Haifa: Bahá'í World Centre, 1976), 28

14. *The Selected Works of Mahatma Gandhi: Volume Four (the Basic Works).* Ed. Shriman Narayan (Ahmedabad: Navajivan Publishing House, 1968), 187.

15. *All Men Are Brothers,* 157.

16. *All Men Are Brothers,* 158.

17. *All Men Are Brothers,* 151.

18. *All Men Are Brothers,* 156

19. *The Promulgation of Universal Peace: Talks Delivered by 'Abdu'l-Bahá during His Visit to the United States and Canada in 1912* (Wilmette: Bahá'í Publishing Trust, 1982), 52–54.

20. *All Men Are Brothers*, 159

21. *Selections from the Writings of 'Abdu'l-Bahá*, 135–6.

22. *Selections from the Writings of 'Abdu'l-Bahá*, 124–25.

23. *All Men Are Brothers*, 158.

24. See, for example, Gandhi's emphasis on education (even for adults) in his *Constructive Programme: Its Meaning and Place*, which may be found in *The Selected Works*.

25. *Kitáb-i-Aqdas*, 37.

26. *The Promise of World Peace*. A statement of the Universal House of Justice addressed to the peoples of the world, dated October 1985.

Chapter 9

Work and Sacrifice

Most people work to make money, so that they can spend it. Is this concept of work adequate for a society that is striving towards a nonviolent civilization founded on spiritual principles? Is money really the best way to motivate work? This chapter examines the concept of work as found in the writings of Gandhi and of the Bahá'í Faith.

9.1 Everyone Must Work

Both Gandhi and the Bahá'ís consider some kind of work to be obligatory. Gandhi writes:

> God created man to work for his food, and said that those who ate without work were thieves.[1]

> The great Nature has intended us to earn our bread in the sweat of our brow. Every one, therefore, who idles away a single minute becomes to that extent a burden upon his neighbors, and to do so is to commit a breach of the very first lesson of *ahimsa*. *Ahimsa* is nothing if not a well-balanced, exquisite consideration for one's neighbor, and an idle man is wanting in that elementary consideration.[2]

Bahá'ís hold similar views. Bahá'u'lláh writes poetically in the *Hidden Words:*

> O My Servants! Ye are the trees of My garden; ye must give forth goodly and wondrous fruits, that ye yourselves and others may profit therefrom. Thus it is incumbent on every one to engage in crafts and professions, for therein lies the secret of wealth, O men of understanding! For results depend upon means, and the grace of God shall be all-sufficient unto you. Trees that yield no fruit have been and will ever be for the fire.[3]

Moreover, in the Kitáb-i-Aqdas, Bahá'u'lláh made work obligatory for Bahá'ís:

> O people of Bahá! It is incumbent upon each one of you to engage in some occupation—such as a craft, a trade or the like. We have exalted your engagement in such work to the rank of worship of the one true God. Reflect, O people, on the grace and blessings of your Lord, and yield Him thanks at eventide and dawn. Waste not your hours in idleness and sloth, but occupy yourselves with what will profit you and others.[4]

The Bahá'í law that everyone must perform some kind of work is further explained by Shoghi Effendi:

> Every individual, no matter how handicapped and limited he may be, is under the obligation of engaging in some work or profession, for work, especially when performed in the spirit of service, is according to Bahá'u'lláh a form of worship. It has not only a utilitarian purpose, but has a value in itself, because it draws us nearer to God, and enables us to better grasp His purpose for us in this world. It is obvious, therefore, that the inheritance of wealth cannot make anyone immune from daily work.[5]

9.2 Mendicancy

Such a work ethic naturally raises the question of unemployed people who, unable to find work, turn to begging. Both Gandhi and the Bahá'ís agree that mendicancy is an unacceptable solution to the problems of the unemployed. Bahá'u'lláh condemns mendicancy:

> The most despised of men in the sight of God are they who sit and beg.[6]

However, in order to be useful, people need to be given skills so that they may be able to earn a living and make themselves useful to society. Concerning this dilemma, Shoghi Effendi writes:

> With reference to Bahá'u'lláh's command concerning the engagement of the believers in some sort of profession: the Teachings are most emphatic on this matter, particularly the statement in the Aqdas to this effect which makes it quite clear that idle people who lack the desire to work can have no place in the new World Order. As a corollary of this principle, Bahá'u'lláh further states that mendicity should not only be discouraged but entirely wiped out from the face of society. It is the duty of those who are in charge of the organization of society to give every individual the opportunity of acquiring the necessary talent in some kind of profession, and also the means of utilizing such a talent, both for its own sake and for the sake of earning the means of his livelihood.[7]

Gandhi held similar views about mendicancy, and felt that it is inconsistent with *Ahimsa:*

> My *Ahimsa* would not tolerate the idea of giving a free meal to a healthy person who has not worked for it in some honest way, and if I had the power, I would stop every *Sadavrat** where free meals are given. It has

---

*Charity.

degraded the nation and has encouraged laziness, idleness, hypocrisy, and even crime. Such misplaced charity adds nothing to the wealth of the country, whether material or spiritual, and gives a false sense of meritoriousness to the donor. How nice it would be if the donors were to open institutions where they would give meals under healthy, clean surroundings to men and women who would work for them... the rule should be, "No labour, no meal"... I know that it is easier to fling free meals in the faces of idlers, but much more difficult to organize an institution where honest work has to be done before meals are served. From a pecuniary standpoint, in the initial stages at any rate, the cost of feeding people after taking work from them will be more than the cost of the present free kitchen. But I am convinced that it will be cheaper in the long run, if we do not want to increase in geometrical progression the race of loafers which is fast over-running this land.[8]

9.3   Work as Worship

The Bahá'í belief that work done in a spirit of service is a form of worship is already apparent in the passage from the Kitáb-i-Aqdas quoted above. 'Abdu'l-Bahá further explains the spiritual dimension of work as follows:

In the Bahá'í Cause arts, sciences and all crafts are counted as worship. The man who makes a piece of notepaper to the best of his ability, conscientiously, concentrating all his forces on perfecting it, is giving praise to God. Briefly, all effort and exertion put forth by man from the fullness of his heart is worship, if it is prompted by the highest motives and the will to do service to humanity. This is worship: to serve mankind and to minister to the needs of the people. Service is prayer. A physician ministering to the sick, gently, tenderly, free from prejudice and believing in the solidarity of the human race, is giving praise.[9]

Similar ideas are found in the writings of Gandhi:

> No work that is done in His name and dedicated to
> Him is small. All work when so done assumes equal
> merit. A scavenger* who works in His service shares
> equal distinction with a king who uses his gifts in His
> name as a mere trustee.[10]

Gandhi believed that helping the poor is an especially good way
to worship God:

> I cannot imagine anything nobler... than that for, say,
> one hour a day, we should all do the labour that the
> poor must do, and thus identify ourselves with them
> and through them with all mankind. I cannot imagine
> better worship of God than that in His name I should
> labour for the poor even as they do.[11]

9.4 Renouncing Reward

Many of Gandhi's writings about work and service revolve around
the concept of *yajña* (YAJ-nya), as it occurs in the *Bhagavad Gita*
(the most famous component of the *Mahabharata* epic, in which
Lord Krishna imparts divine knowledge to his friend and pupil
Arjuna). *Yajña* is a Sanskrit word which means "sacrifice." According to Gandhi's interpretation of the *Gita*, the best sacrifice is
the one performed with the purest motive and with no desire for
reward. Gandhi taught that we must renounce the fruit of action
and believed that any work, service, or duty performed with detached hearts and pure motives is a form of *yajña*. The concept of
yajña thus constitutes the philosophical kernel of Gandhi's work
ethic. Accordingly, a brief discussion of *yajña* follows. Gandhi
writes about *yajña* as follows:

> *Yajña* means an act directed to the welfare of others,
> done without desiring any return for it, whether of a
> temporal or spiritual nature. 'Act' here must be taken

---

*An untouchable who manually clears faeces from public and private latrines and disposes of carcasses. See also the discussion in Section 6.3.

in its widest sense, and includes thought and word, as well as deed. 'Others' embraces not only humanity, but all life...

Again, a primary sacrifice must be an act which conduces the most to the welfare of the greatest number in the widest area, and which can be performed by the largest number of men and women with the least trouble. It will not, therefore, be a *yajña*, much less a *mahayajña*, to wish or do ill to anyone else, even in order to serve a so-called higher interest. And the Gita teaches and experience testifies that all action that cannot come under the category of *yajña* promotes bondage.

The world cannot subsist for a single moment without *yajña* in this sense, and therefore, the Gita after having dealt with true wisdom in the second chapter, takes up in the third the means of attaining it, and declares in so many words that *yajña* came with the Creation itself. This body, therefore, has been given us only in order that we may serve all Creation with it. And therefore, says the Gita, he who eats without offering *yajña* eats stolen food. Every single act of one who would lead a life of purity should be in the nature of *yajña*.

Yajña having come to us with our birth, we are debtors all our lives, and thus for ever bound to serve the universe. And even as a bondslave receives food, clothing and so on from the master whom he serves, so should we gratefully accept such gifts as may be assigned to us by the Lord of the universe. What we receive must be called a gift; for as debtors we are entitled to no consideration for the discharge of our obligations. Therefore, we may not blame the Master, if we fail to get it. Our body is His to be cherished or cast away according to His will.

This is not a matter for complaint or even pity; on the contrary, it is natural and even a pleasant and desirable state if only we realize our proper place in God's

scheme. We do, indeed, need strong faith if we would
experience this supreme bliss. "Do not worry in the
least about yourself, leave all worry to God,"—this appears to be the commandment in all religions.

This need not frighten anyone. He who devotes himself to service with a clear conscience will day by day
grasp the necessity for it in greater measure, and will
continually grow richer in faith. The path of service
can hardly be trodden by one who is not prepared to
renounce self-interest, and to recognize the conditions
of his birth. Consciously or unconsciously, every one
of us does render some service or other. If we cultivate
the habit of doing this service deliberately, our desire
for service will steadily grow stronger, and will make
not only for our own happiness, but that of the world
at large.[12]

There are two points in Gandhi's exposition of the concept of
yajña above that are also found in the Bahá'í writings, namely,
(i) that everyone is capable of performing worship, *yajña,* or sacrifice through work performed in the spirit of service, and (ii) that
the best and highest form of sacrifice is the one carried out with
the least desire for reward. The first of these two points has already been discussed above, while the second point is considered
below.

Bahá'u'lláh teaches that although God has ordained a recompense for every deed, nevertheless the truly wise do not seek the
fruit of their actions, but rather base their deeds on pure, unselfish
motives:

For every act performed there shall be a recompense
according to the estimate of God, and unto this the
very ordinances and prohibitions prescribed by the
Almighty amply bear witness. For surely if deeds were
not rewarded and yielded no fruit, then the Cause of
God—exalted is He—would prove futile. Immeasurably high is He exalted above such blasphemies! However, unto them that are rid of all attachments a deed
is, verily, its own reward. Were We to enlarge upon this

theme numerous Tablets would need to be written.[13]

Moreover, the idea that the highest worship is the one performed without regard to reward or punishment is found in the earliest sacred texts of the Bahá'í Faith. The Báb, in setting down the standard for worship, wrote:

> Worship thou God in such wise that if thy worship lead thee to the fire, no alteration in thine adoration would be produced, and so likewise if thy recompense should be paradise. Thus and thus alone should be the worship which befitteth the one True God. Shouldst thou worship Him because of fear, this would be unseemly in the sanctified Court of His presence, and could not be regarded as an act by thee dedicated to the Oneness of His Being. Or if thy gaze should be on paradise, and thou shouldst worship Him while cherishing such a hope, thou wouldst make God's creation a partner with Him, notwithstanding the fact that paradise is desired by men.

> Fire and paradise both bow down and prostrate themselves before God. That which is worthy of His Essence is to worship Him for His sake, without fear of fire, or hope of paradise.

> Although when true worship is offered, the worshipper is delivered from the fire, and entereth the paradise of God's good-pleasure, yet such should not be the motive of his act. However, God's favour and grace ever flow in accordance with the exigencies of His inscrutable wisdom.[14]

9.5 The Ideal of Service

In summary, both Gandhi and the Bahá'ís agree that worship of God through service of humanity is the ultimate goal of work. Gandhi writes:

> *Yajña* is duty to be performed, or service to be rendered, all the twenty-four hours of the day... To serve

without desire is to favour not others, but ourselves,
even as in discharging a debt we serve only ourselves,
lighten our burden and fulfil our duty. Again, not only
the good, but all of us are bound to place our resources
at the disposal of humanity. And if such is the law,
as evidently it is, indulgence ceases to hold a place in
life and gives way to renunciation. The duty of renunciation differentiates mankind from the beast... But
renunciation here does not mean abandoning the world
and retiring to the forest. The spirit of renunciation
should rule all the activities of life.[15]

Man's ultimate aim is the realization of God, and all
his activities, social, political, and religious, have to
be guided by the ultimate aim of the vision of God.
The immediate service of all human beings becomes
a necessary part of the endeavour simply because the
only way to find God is to see Him in His creation and
be one with it. This can only be done by service of
all.[16]

This topic is sufficiently important to the Bahá'ís that it is
discussed in a statement on social and economic issues prepared
in 1995 by the Bahá'í International Community's Office of Public Information titled *The Prosperity of Humankind,* and used by
the Bahá'ís to help interact with governments, organizations, and
people everywhere:

In most of contemporary thinking, the concept of work
has been largely reduced to that of gainful employment
aimed at acquiring the means for the consumption of
available goods. The system is circular: acquisition and
consumption resulting in the maintenance and expan-
sion of the production of goods and, in consequence, in
supporting paid employment. Taken individually, all of
these activities are essential to the well-being of society.
The inadequacy of the overall conception, however, can
be read in both the apathy that social commentators
discern among large numbers of the employed in every

land and the demoralization of the growing armies of the unemployed.

Not surprisingly, therefore, there is increasing recognition that the world is in urgent need of a new "work ethic". Here again, nothing less than insights generated by the creative interaction of the scientific and religious systems of knowledge can produce so fundamental a reorientation of habits and attitudes. Unlike animals, .which depend for their sustenance on whatever the environment readily affords, human beings are impelled to express the immense capacities latent within them through productive work designed to meet their own needs and those of others. In acting thus they become participants, at however modest a level, in the processes of the advancement of civilization. They fulfill purposes that unite them with others. To the extent that work is consciously undertaken in a spirit of service to humanity, Bahá'u'lláh says, it is a form of prayer, a means of worshiping God. Every individual has the capacity to see himself or herself in this light, and it is to this inalienable capacity of the self that development strategy must appeal, whatever the nature of the plans being pursued, whatever the rewards they promise. No narrower a perspective will ever call up from the people of the world the magnitude of effort and commitment that the economic tasks ahead will require.[17]

Chapter Notes

1. *The Mind of Mahatma Gandhi*. Ed. R. K. Prabhu and U. R. Rao (Ahmedabad: Navajivan Publishing House, 1967), 198.

2. *The Mind of Mahatma Gandhi*, 198

3. *The Hidden Words of Bahá'u'lláh.* Trans. Shoghi Effendi (Wilmette: Bahá'í Publishing Trust, 1985), 51.

4. *Kitáb-i-Aqdas* (Haifa: Bahá'í World Centre, 1992), 30.

5. Shoghi Effendi, quoted in *Kitáb-i-Aqdas* (Haifa: Bahá'í World Centre, 1992), 192.

6. *Kitáb-i-Aqdas*, 30.

7. Shoghi Effendi, quoted in *Kitáb-i-Aqdas* (Haifa: Bahá'í World Centre, 1992), 192.

8. *The Mind of Mahatma Gandhi*, 195.

9. 'Abdu'l-Bahá, quoted in J. E. Esslemont, *Bahá'u'lláh and the New Era*, 5th rev. ed. (Wilmette: Bahá'í Publishing Trust, 1987), 79.

10. *The Mind of Mahatma Gandhi*, 202.

11. *The Mind of Mahatma Gandhi*, 202.

12. *The Mind of Mahatma Gandhi*, 228–9.

13. *Tablets of Bahá'u'lláh Revealed after the Kitáb-i-Aqdas* (Wilmette: Bahá'í Publishing Trust, 1988), 189.

14. *Selections from the Writings of the Báb* (Haifa: Bahá'í World Centre, 1982), 77–8.

15. *The Mind of Mahatma Gandhi*, 229–30.

16. *The Mind of Mahatma Gandhi*, 224.

17. *The Prosperity Of Humankind*, A statement prepared by the Bahá'í International Community's Office of Public Information.

Chapter 10

Humanizing the Economy

Our present civilization rests on an economic structure that is fundamentally unsound. There is more food, money, and goods today than there has ever been in history, yet poverty is far from being eliminated. Although the world's population is large, it is not so large that people need to go hungry or forego basic health care, basic education, etc. With famine, for example, the problem has been the politics of food distribution, not a scarcity of food. Today we have a strange situation in which a tiny fraction of the world's population owns and controls almost everything material, while the majority of people have to struggle and split the small remainder that is left. That there is something fundamentally wrong with our economic model can also be seen from the following bewildering fact: Even though machines and computers save a huge amount of time and money, people today are nevertheless working longer hours per day on average than before the industrial revolution—before the invention of machines.[1] It is truly ironic: we have machines that can do the work of a thousand individuals, yet people are working more today than before machines were invented! To make matters even worse, especially in the "developed" world, millions of people are unemployed while at the same time those in paid work are working longer hours! How can this be?

The industrial system appears to have failed in the task of sharing the available work—and leisure time for family life and community service—equitably.

Our present economic model relies on consumption to stimulate demand for goods, services, etc., thereby leading to the creation of employment opportunities. This is a self-perpetuating system, and as such, will likely not collapse like some communist economies did. However, this economic system is fundamentally amoral, i.e., "you get out what you put in" as far as values and principles are concerned. The system merely reflects our values. While this is not a bad thing in itself, it means that there is no objective, pre-determined way to assign value to goods, services, etc. Prices are set based on the values that people assign to them—ultimately, by the values and principles people uphold and cherish. Currently, our values glorify material pursuits above all else, hence we are living in an age of inverted priorities, in which people sometimes even outbid each other to *pay* more money to harm themselves and others (with "recreational" drugs, for example). Money pre-vails over principle. Fortunately, this sad state of affairs is slowly changing, partially because today's economy is generating sorrow and discontent on a massive, "planetary" scale. Since happiness and contentment are not material objects, therefore they have no associated material price. Hence, the current global economy effec-tively ignores them altogether, trampling over whatever it cannot set a price on—the environment, people's wellbeing, and ethics, for example. The end result? Neither the rich nor the poor are really happy. Ultimately, our economic problems stem from a crisis of values and principles, therefore their solution must reside outside our current value system. Essentially, we need spiritual solutions for economic problems. This idea can be found in the writing of both Gandhi and of the Bahá'í Faith.

10.1   Equitable Wealth Distribution

One of the principal economic goals of both Gandhi and the Bahá'ís concerns the elimination of the extremes of poverty and wealth. 'Abdu'l-Bahá explains,

The arrangements of the circumstances of the people must be such that poverty shall disappear, that everyone, as far as possible, according to his rank and position, shall share in comfort and well-being. We see among us men who are overburdened with riches on the one hand, and on the other those unfortunate ones who starve with nothing; those who possess several stately palaces, and those who have not where to lay their head. Some we find with numerous courses of costly and dainty food; whilst others can scarce find sufficient crusts to keep them alive. Whilst some are clothed in velvets, furs and fine linen, others have insufficient, poor and thin garments with which to protect them from the cold. This condition of affairs is wrong, and must be remedied.[2]

Similar ideas are found in the writings of Gandhi:

The rich have a superfluous store of things which they do not need, and which are therefore neglected and wasted, while millions are starved to death for want of sustenance... As it is, the rich are discontented no less than the poor. The poor man would fain become a millionaire, and the millionaire a multimillionaire.[3]

10.2 Economic Equality Unattainable

The Bahá'ís, like Gandhi, recognize the urgent need for reform in the economic relations of rich and poor and for the elimination of the extremes of poverty and wealth. Both agree, however, that an equal distribution of wealth is impractical, and that attempts to impose equality only betray a deep misunderstanding of human nature.

'Abdu'l-Bahá explains the futility of forceful imposition of equality as a solution for our economic problems:

Now the remedy must be carefully undertaken. It cannot be done by bringing to pass absolute equality between men. Equality is a chimera! It is entirely imprac-

ticable. Even if equality could be achieved it could not
continue; and if its existence were possible, the whole
order of the world would be destroyed. The Law of
Order must always obtain in the world of humanity.
Heaven has so decreed in the creation of man... Humanity, like a great army, requires a general, captains,
underofficers in their degree, and soldiers, each with
their appointed duties. Degrees are absolutely necessary to ensure an orderly organization. An army could
not be composed of generals alone, or of captains only,
or of nothing but soldiers without anyone in authority.[4]

Gandhi felt similarly, and writes,

I cannot picture to myself a time when no man shall be
richer than another. But I do picture a time when the
rich will spurn to enrich themselves at the expense of
the poor and the poor will cease to envy the rich. Even
in a most perfect world, we shall fail to avoid inequalities, but we can and must avoid strife and bitterness.[5]

My ideal is equal distribution, but insofar as I can see,
it is not to be realized. I therefore work for equitable
distribution.[6]

10.3   Collective Trusteeship

Bahá'ís believe that although social laws may be needed for the
regulation of wealth, our worldwide economic problems are essentially spiritual in origin. At the core of Bahá'í thinking on economic
problems lies the concept of trusteeship. Bahá'u'lláh writes in the
Hidden Words:

O Ye Rich Ones On Earth!
The poor in your midst are My trust; guard ye My
trust, and be not intent only on your own ease.[7]

The same principle of trusteeship may be found in Gandhi's
writings:

We invite the capitalist to regard himself as a trustee
for those on whom he depends for the making, the re-
tention, and the increase of his capital.[8]

Those who own money now are asked to behave like
the trustees holding their riches on behalf of the poor.
You may say that trusteeship is a legal fiction. But,
if people meditate over it constantly and try to act up
to it, then life on earth would be governed far more
by love than it is at present. Absolute trusteeship is
an abstraction like Euclid's definition of a point, and
is equally unattainable. But if we strive for it, we shall
be able to go further in realizing a state of equality on
earth than by any other method.[9]

The next few pages explore key facets of this important principle, as described in the writings of Gandhi and of the Bahá'í
Faith.

10.4   The Wellbeing of the Whole

Bahá'ís believe that since humankind is an organic whole, therefore any advantage gained by one segment of society at the expense of another is of no lasting benefit to the overall wellbeing
of humankind.* Indeed, the disadvantages may far outweigh any
advantages gained. This idea, central as it is to Bahá'í economic
thinking, can be found further explained in *The Prosperity of Humankind*.[10] Here are some excerpts:

In a letter addressed to Queen Victoria over a century
ago, and employing an analogy that points to the one
model holding convincing promise for the organisation
of a planetary society, Bahá'u'lláh compared the world
to the human body. There is, indeed, no other model in
phenomenal existence to which we can reasonably look.
Human society is composed not of a mass of merely dif-
ferentiated cells but of associations of individuals, each
one of whom is endowed with intelligence and will...

---

*See also Section 6.2.

Since the body of humankind is one and indivisible, each member of the race is born into the world as a trust of the whole. This trusteeship constitutes the moral foundation of most of the other rights—principally economic and social—which the instruments of the United Nations are attempting similarly to define. The security of the family and the home, the ownership of property, and the right to privacy are all implied in such a trusteeship. The obligations on the part of the community extend to the provision of employment, mental and physical health care, social security, fair wages, rest and recreation, and a host of other reasonable expectations on the part of the individual members of society.

The principle of collective trusteeship creates also the right of every person to expect that those cultural conditions essential to his or her identity enjoy the protection of national and international law. Much like the role played by the gene pool in the biological life of humankind and its environment, the immense wealth of cultural diversity achieved over thousands of years is vital to the social and economic development of a human race experiencing its collective coming-of-age. It represents a heritage that must be permitted to bear its fruit in a global civilization. On the one hand, cultural expressions need to be protected from suffocation by the materialistic influences currently holding sway. On the other, cultures must be enabled to interact with one another in ever-changing patterns of civilization, free of manipulation for partisan political ends.

Today, in an era most of whose pressing problems are global in nature, persistence in the idea that power means advantage for various segments of the human family is profoundly mistaken in theory and of no practical service to the social and economic development of the planet.

The analogy of the human body with the body of humankind

can also be found in Gandhi's writings. Writing about the inequalities of wealth generated in capitalism, Gandhi explains:

... the beneficialness of the inequality depends first, on the methods by which it was accomplished and secondly, on the purposes to which it is applied. Inequalities of wealth, unjustly established, have assuredly injured the nation in which they exist during their establishment; and unjustly directed, injure it yet more during their existence. But inequalities of wealth, justly established, benefit the nation in the course of their establishment; and nobly used, aid it yet more by their existence.

Thus the circulation of wealth in a nation resembles that of the blood in the natural body. There is one quickness of the current which comes of cheerful emotion or wholesome exercise; and another which comes of shame or fever. There is a flush of the body which is full of warmth and life; and another which will pass into putrefaction.

Again even as the diseased local determination of the blood involves depression of the general health of the system, all morbid local action of riches will be found ultimately to involve a weakening of the resources of the body politic.[11]

10.5 Eliminating Exploitation

Bahá'ís believe that economic exploitation of the poor by the rich is wrong. When in the United States in 1912, 'Abdu'l-Bahá said to the American people:

Between 1860 and 1865 you did a wonderful thing; you abolished chattel slavery; but today you must do a much more wonderful thing: you must abolish industrial slavery.

The solution of economic questions will not be brought about by array of capital against labor, and labor against capital, in strife and conflict, but by the voluntary attitude of goodwill on both sides. Then a real and lasting justness of conditions will be secured...

Among the Bahá'ís there are no extortionate, mercenary and unjust practices, no rebellious demands, no revolutionary uprisings against existing governments...

It will not be possible in the future for men to amass great fortunes by the labors of others. The rich will willingly divide. They will come to this gradually, naturally, by their own volition. It will never be accomplished by war and bloodshed.[12]

Gandhi was even more emphatic in condemning the legal exploitation of disadvantaged people. Gandhi writes rhetorically about the free market:

So far as I know, there is not in history record of anything so disgraceful to the human intellect as the modern idea that the commercial text 'Buy in the cheapest market and sell in the dearest' represents an available principle of national economy. Buy in the cheapest market? —yes; but what made your market cheap? Charcoal may be cheap among your roof timbers after a fire and bricks may be cheap after an earthquake; but fire and earthquake may not therefore be national benefits. Sell in the dearest? —yes, truly; but what made your market dear? You sold your bread well today: was it to a dying man who gave his last coin for it and will never need bread more; or to a rich man who tomorrow will buy your farm over your head; or to a soldier on his way to pillage the bank in which you have put your fortune?

None of these things you can know. One thing only you can know; namely whether this dealing of yours is a just and faithful one, which is all you need concern yourself...[13]

10.6   Laws to Regulate Wealth

Both Gandhi and the Bahá'ís agree that social laws are necessary to reduce the inordinate disparity between rich and poor and especially to eliminate economic exploitation. 'Abdu'l-Bahá writes,

> Certainly, some being enormously rich and other lamentably poor, an organization is necessary to control and improve this state of affairs. It is important to limit riches, as it is also of importance to limit poverty. Either extreme is not good... When we see poverty allowed to reach a condition of starvation, it is a sure sign that somewhere we shall find tyranny. Men must bestir themselves in this matter, and no longer delay in altering conditions which bring the misery of grinding poverty to a very large number of people.
>
> The rich must give of their abundance; they must soften their hearts and cultivate a compassionate intelligence, taking thought for those sad ones who are suffering from lack of the very necessaries of life.
>
> There must be special laws made, dealing with these extremes of rich and want... The government of the countries should conform to the Divine Law which gives equal justice to all... Not until this is done will the Law of God be obeyed.[14]

Gandhi, explaining the need for laws regulating the flow and distribution of wealth, writes,

> The flowing of streams is in one respect a perfect image of the action of wealth. Where land falls, the water flows. So wealth must go where it is required. But the disposition and administration of rivers can be altered by human forethought. Whether the stream shall be a curse or a blessing depends upon man's labour and administrating intelligence. For centuries districts of the world, rich in soil and favoured in climate, have lain desert under the rage of their own rivers; not only desert, but plague-struck. The stream which, rightly

directed, would have flowed in soft irrigation from field
to field—would have purified the air, given food to
man and beast, and carried their burdens for them on
its bosom—now overwhelms the plain and poisons the
wind; its breath pestilence, and its work famine. In
like manner human laws can guide the flow of wealth.
This the leading trench and limiting mound can do so
thoroughly that it shall become [the] water of life—the
riches of the hand of wisdom; or on [the] contrary, by
leaving it to its own lawless flow, they may make it
the last and deadliest of natural plagues: [the] water of
Marah*—the water which feeds the roots of all evil.[15]

10.7   The Root of the Problem

Because today's economic problems are essentially spiritual in origin, what we need is a new understanding of wealth guided by
the spiritual principles of justice and the oneness of humankind.
Today, most employers pay their employees only with wages. However, as society learns to assign a spiritual as well as material value
to work, it will become possible for people and organizations to
measure their incomes not only by how much money they make,
but also by how much they have served humanity. This subject is
also covered in another chapter.†

Explaining the inadequacy of money to motivate people to work
cooperatively, 'Abdu'l-Bahá explained as far back as in 1912:

Now I want to tell you about the law of God. According to the divine law, employees should not be paid
merely by wages. Nay, rather they should be partners
in every work. The question of socialization is very
difficult. It will not be solved by strikes for wages.
All the governments of the world must be united, and
organize an assembly, the members of which shall be
elected from the parliaments and the noble ones of the
nations. These must plan with wisdom and power, so

*See Exodus 15:23.The Hebrew word for Marah means "bitter."
†See Chapter 9.

that neither the capitalists suffer enormous losses, nor
the laborers become needy. In the utmost moderation
they should make the law, then announce to the public
that the rights of the working people are to be effec-
tively preserved; also the rights of the capitalists are
to be protected. When such a general law is adopted,
by the will of both sides, should a strike occur, all the
governments of the world should collectively resist it.
Otherwise the work will lead to much destruction, especially in Europe. Terrible things will take place...
The owners of properties, mines and factories, should
share their incomes with their employees, and give a
fairly certain percentage of their profits to their working men, in order that the employees should receive,
besides their wages, some of the general income of the
factory, so that the employee may strive with his soul
in the work.[16]

Gandhi also advocated rewarding good work with more than
wages:

Modern political economy... imagines that man has a
body but no soul to be taken into account and frames
its laws accordingly. How can such laws possibly apply
to man in whom the soul is the predominant element?
... We see how helpless it is when labourers go on a
strike. The masters take one view of the matter, the
operatives another; and no political economy can set
them at one. Disputant after disputant vainly strives
to show that the interests of the masters are not antagonistic to those of the men. In fact it does not always
follow that the persons must be antagonistic because
their interests are. If there is only a crust of bread in
the house, and the mother and children are starving,
their interests are not the same. If the mother eats it,
the children want it; if the children eat it, the mother
must go hungry to her work. Yet it does not follow that
there is antagonism between them, that they will fight
for the crust, and the mother, being strongest, will get

it and eat it. Similarly it cannot be assumed that because their interests are diverse, persons must regard
one another with hostility and use violence or cunning
to obtain the advantage.

Even if we consider men as actuated by no other moral
influences than those which affect rats or swine, it can
never be shown generally either that the interests of
master and labourer are alike or that they are opposed;
for according to circumstances they may be either...

I have meant in the term justice to include affection—
such affection as one man *owes* to another. All right
relations between master and operative ultimately depend on this.

As an illustration, let us consider the position of domestic servants.

We will suppose that the master of a household tries
only to get as much work out of his servants as he can,
at the rate of wages he gives. He never allows them to
be idle; feeds them as poorly and lodges them as ill as
they will endure. In doing this, there is no violation on
his part of what is commonly called 'justice'. He agrees
with the domestic for his whole time and service and
takes them, the limits of hardship in treatment being
fixed by the practice of other masters in the neighbor-
hood. If the servant can get a better place, he is free
to take one.

This is the politico-economical view of the case according to the doctors of that science who assert that by
this procedure the greatest average of work will be obtained from the servant, and therefore the greatest benefit to the community, and through the community, to
the servant himself.

That however is not so. It would be so if the servant
were an engine of which the motive power was steam,
magnetism, or some such agent of calculable force. But
on the contrary he is an engine whose motive power

is the Soul. Soul force enters into all the economist's equations without his knowledge and falsifies every one of their results. The largest quantity of work will not be done by this curious engine for pay or under pressure. It will be done when the motive force, that it to say, the will or spirit of the creature, is brought to its greatest strength by its own proper fuel, namely by the affections.[17]

One logical consequence of the spiritual principle of the oneness of humankind is that we help ourselves by helping others, but harm ourselves by harming others. Thus, we find in many of the Bahá'í writings references to a future time when people will, of their own free volition, wish to share their wealth with others. In a letter to the Central Organization for a Durable Peace, written in 1919, 'Abdu'l-Bahá explained,

> Among the teachings of Bahá'u'lláh is voluntary sharing of one's property with others among mankind. This voluntary sharing is greater than (legally imposed) equality, and consists in this, that one should not prefer oneself to others, but rather should sacrifice one's life and property for others. But this should not be introduced by coercion so that it becomes a law which man is compelled to follow. Nay, rather, man should voluntarily and of his own choice sacrifice his property and life for others, and spend willingly for the poor, just as is done in Persia among the Bahá'ís.[18]

Gandhi also considered voluntary sharing to be a necessary part of trusteeship:

> A non-violent system of government is clearly an impossibility so long as the wide gulf between the rich and the hungry millions persists... A violent and bloody revolution is a certainty one day unless there is a voluntary abdication of riches and the power that riches give and sharing them for the common good. I adhere to my doctrine of trusteeship in spite of the ridicule that has been poured upon it. It is true that it is difficult to reach. So is non-violence difficult to attain.[19]

10.8   Social and Economic Justice

Nonviolence is manifested most visibly at the level of the individuals in attributes such as forgiveness, compassion, and mercy. However, the expression of nonviolence at the societal level, it may be argued, requires that justice reign supreme. Gandhi felt that unless justice and spiritual values are re-introduced into our economic relations, there can be no lasting solution to the many ills afflicting society. He writes,

> True economics is the economics of justice. People will be happy in so far as they learn to do justice and righteousness. All else is not only vain but leads straight to destruction. To teach the people to get rich by hook or by crook is to do them an immense disservice.[20]

> That economics is untrue which ignores or disregards moral values. The extension of the law of non-violence in the domain of economics means nothing less than the introduction of moral values as a factor to be considered in regulating international commerce.[21]

Bahá'ís believe that justice is vital to society, and it is no mere accident that the supreme ruling body of the Bahá'í Faith is named *The Universal House of Justice*. What exactly is justice? Because of its relevance to today's economic and social problems (and their solution), this question is discussed in *The Prosperity of Humankind:*[10]

> Justice is the one power that can translate the dawning consciousness of humanity's oneness into a collective will through which the necessary structures of global community life can be confidently erected. An age that sees the people of the world increasingly gaining access to information of every kind and to a diversity of ideas will find justice asserting itself as the ruling principle of successful social organisation. With ever greater frequency, proposals aiming at the development of the planet will have to submit to the candid light of the standards it requires...

At the group level, a concern for justice is the indispensable compass in collective decision making, because it is the only means by which unity of thought and action can be achieved. Far from encouraging the punitive spirit that has often masqueraded under its name in past ages, justice is the practical expression of awareness that, in the achievement of human progress, the interests of the individual and those of society are inextricably linked. To the extent that justice becomes a guiding concern of human interaction, a consultative climate is encouraged that permits options to be examined dispassionately and appropriate courses of action selected. In such a climate the perennial tendencies toward manipulation and partisanship are far less likely to deflect the decision-making process.

The implications for social and economic development are profound. Concern for justice protects the task of defining progress from the temptation to sacrifice the well-being of the generality of humankind—and even of the planet itself—-to the advantages which technological breakthroughs can make available to privileged minorities. In design and planning, it ensures that limited resources are not diverted to the pursuit of projects extraneous to a community's essential social or economic priorities. Above all, only development programmes that are perceived as meeting their needs and as being just and equitable in objective can hope to engage the commitment of the masses of humanity, upon whom implementation depends. The relevant human qualities such as honesty, a willingness to work, and a spirit of co-operation are successfully harnessed to the accomplishment of enormously demanding collective goals when every member of society—indeed every component group within society—can trust that they are protected by standards and assured of benefits that apply equally to all.[10]

Justice, then, is the key to transforming our pathologically materialistic economic system into one that is healthy and sound.

Chapter Notes

1. The question of working hours before the industrial revolution is somwhat controversial, for fairly obvious reasons. Most of the evidence indicates that workers in pre-industrial societies had—and have—far more leisure time than workers in industrial societies. The scientific evidence consists largely of records of paid workers, as well as information on the number of religious holidays enjoyed during pre-industrial times in Europe. A considerable amount of evidence on the issue has been assembled by Schor. See, for example, J. B. Schor, *The Overworked American: The Unexpected Decline of Leisure* (New York: Basic Books, 1991).

2. 'Abdu'l-Bahá, *Paris Talks* (London: Bahá'í Publishing Trust, 1972), 151.

3. *All Men Are Brothers: Life and Thoughts of Mahatma Gandhi as Told in His Own Words.* Ed. K Kripalani (Paris: UNESCO, 1969), 131.

4. 'Abdu'l-Bahá, quoted in J. E. Esslemont, *Bahá'u'lláh and the New Era,* 5th rev. ed. (Wilmette: Bahá'í Publishing Trust, 1987), 140–1.

5. *All Men Are Brothers,* 136.

6. *All Men Are Brothers,* 129.

7. *The Hidden Words of Bahá'u'lláh.* Trans. Shoghi Effendi (Wilmette: Bahá'í Publishing Trust, 1985), 41.

8. *The Mind of Mahatma Gandhi.* Ed. R. K. Prabhu and U. R. Rao (Ahmedabad: Navajivan Publishing House, 1967), 135.

9. *All Men Are Brothers,* 137.

10. *The Prosperity Of Humankind,* A statement prepared by the Bahá'í International Community's Office of Public Information and used by the Bahá'ís to help interact with governments, organizations, and people everywhere.

11. *The Selected Works of Mahatma Gandhi: Volume Four (the Basic Works).* Ed. Shriman Narayan (Ahmedabad: Navajivan Publishing House, 1968), 59–60.

12. 'Abdu'l-Bahá, quoted in *Bahá'u'lláh and the New Era,* 144–5.

13. *The Selected Works of Mahatma Gandhi: Volume Four,* 65–6.

14. 'Abdu'l-Bahá, quoted in *Bahá'u'lláh and the New Era,* 141.

15. *The Selected Works of Mahatma Gandhi: Volume Four*, 69.
16. 'Abdu'l-Bahá, quoted in *Bahá'u'lláh and the New Era*, 145–6.
17. *The Selected Works of Mahatma Gandhi: Volume Four*, 44–7.
18. 'Abdu'l-Bahá, quoted in *Bahá'u'lláh and the New Era*, 142.
19. *All Men Are Brothers*, 131.
20. *The Selected Works of Mahatma Gandhi: Volume Four*, 73.
21. *All Men Are Brothers*, 129.

Chapter 11

Politics and Social Change

Previous chapters have examined aspects of the Gandhian and the Bahá'í visions of a nonviolent world. However, a vision is useless unless we strive towards it, and striving, in turn, implies the channelling of human volition through appropriate means. What are these means? How should we go about trying to change the social, economic and political state of affairs?

Our current model of politics and social transformation has its origins many centuries ago. A simplified view of our contemporary political framework is that its "political machinery" serves the purpose of balancing the "power struggle" between the conflicting interests of opposing parties: of the state and of the individuals it comprises, capital and labor, etc. Democracy is supposed to work by bringing about an "equilibrium," so that if one party becomes too powerful then the politics shifts in the other direction. This model is loosely inspired by the physics of the pendulum, studied by Galileo Galilei in the dark days when Europeans could not openly (and safely) say that the earth was not the center of the solar system. The "political pendulum," as it "swings left and right" will "gravitate" back towards the "political center" (equilibrium point) that best balances the interests of the individual and the state—or else of capital and of labour, etc. But a pendulum is an extremely simple physical system with very limited degrees of freedom: it can swing, however it cannot do much else. In contrast, human politics—not party politics—is an extremely complex process whose dynamics is far richer than the relatively pathetic swinging motion of the pendulum. If science has advanced far beyond the physics of the pendulum, then it is only to be expected that new ways of thinking can also be found in politics. Sadly, our political institutions and the way they function have not changed on any fundamental level for the past few centuries.

One of the greatest, most serious problems with the current political model is that it assumes that the "right" and the "left" are in a perpetual power struggle. Hence, politics is reduced to balancing the supposedly conflicting interests. This thinking fundamentally contradicts the principle of the oneness of humankind: if humankind is a single organism, then the interests of its different parts must necessarily harmonize with the interests of the whole— and therefore of other parts. But instead of trying to serve the interests of the whole of humankind, our current political system fuels a never-ending, artificial struggle between different segments of society. This bipolar political system is inherently violent, so it cannot serve as the foundation for a truly nonviolent civilization. Indeed, it can never transcend the power struggle.

Multi-party politics fares no better, in this sense, than does the two-party system. What then should we do? As discussed in greater detail in Chapter 5, Gandhi and the Bahá'ís both agree that a nonviolent civilization must have as its basis a nonviolent political system. Specifically, power structures must become decentralized* and the military model of rigidly one-way, top-down, hierarchical organizations must yield to the democratic spirit[†]. This chapter further explores what Gandhi and the Bahá'ís have to say about politics and social transformation.

---

*See also Section 5.4
[†]See also Section 5.5

11.1 Gandhian and Bahá'í Methods

It is instructive to consider and compare the methods used by Bahá'ís and by Gandhi to promote social change. Neither of them have resorted to armies, terrorism, sabotage or clandestine activities. Both of them have succeeded in achieving their aims using, what may be broadly termed, nonviolent methods.* But beyond this general similarity lie a number of differences. Gandhi's specific objective was to secure political autonomy and independence for his countrymen. This goal is vastly different from the aims of the Bahá'í Faith. Hence, it should not surprise the reader that since the founding of the Bahá'í Faith in 1863, the Bahá'ís have used methods that are even less socially disruptive—hence less violent—than those used by Gandhi.

For instance, Gandhi considered it necessary to resort to nonviolent civil disobedience as a last, extreme measure when less disruptive methods had been tried and failed. An example of Gandhi's political genius is his famous salt march, in which he skillfully used nonviolent civil disobedience as a highly effective instrument for raising awareness, ultimately resulting in the desired political and social change. Gandhi's disobedience often landed him in jail, from where he further grew in stature and political power. Notwithstanding Gandhi's many successes, his nonviolent civil disobedience was disobedience nonetheless. Although Gandhi understood the danger of civil disobedience to society, his rhetoric maintained that there was greater danger in doing nothing:

> A good man will therefore resist an evil system or administration with his whole soul. Disobedience of the law of an evil State is therefore a duty... Non-violent, i.e., civil, disobedience is the only and most successful remedy and is obligatory upon him who would dissociate himself from evil.

> There is danger in civil disobedience only because it is still only a partially tried remedy and has always to be tried in an atmosphere surcharged with violence. For when tyranny is rampant much rage is generated

---

*See also Section 5.3.

among the victims. It remains latent because of their
weakness and bursts in all its fury on the slightest pretext. Civil disobedience is a sovereign method of trans-
muting this undisciplined life-destroying latent energy
into disciplined life-saving energy whose use ensures absolute success.[1]

In contrast, Bahá'ís have had a century-long history of obedience to
even extremely oppressive and unjust governments. Bahá'ís have
never engaged in any form of organized civil disobedience. The
reason for this difference of approach is that Gandhi's immediate
political goal was to secure some level of self-government. In contrast the Bahá'ís have no interest in any political objective beyond
uniting and serving humankind, even if it becomes necessary at
times to submit to the authority of tyrannical and merciless authorities. Esslemont gives an illustrative example of the Bahá'í
approach towards nonviolent obedience to governments:

> In bringing about the emancipation of women as in
> other matters, Bahá'u'lláh counsels His followers to
> avoid methods of violence. An excellent illustration
> of the Bahá'í method of social reform has been given
> by the Bahá'í in Persia, Egypt and Syria. In these
> countries it is customary for Muhammadan [Muslim]
> women outside their homes to wear a veil covering the
> face. The Báb indicated that in the New Dispensation
> women would be relieved from this irksome restraint,
> but Bahá'u'lláh counsels His followers, where no im-
> portant question of morality is involved, to defer to
> established customs until people become enlightened,
> rather than scandalize those amongst whom they live,
> and arouse needless antagonism. The Bahá'í women,
> therefore, although well aware that the antiquated cus-
> tom of wearing the veil is, for enlightened people, un-
> necessary and inconvenient, yet quietly put up with the
> inconvenience, rather than rouse a storm of fanatical
> hatred and rancorous opposition by uncovering their
> faces in public. This conformity to custom is in no way
> due to fear, but to an assured confidence in the power

of education and in the transforming and life-giving effect of true religion. Bahá'ís in these regions are devoting their energies to the education of their children, especially their girls, and to the diffusion and promotion of the Bahá'í ideals, well knowing that as the new spiritual life grows and spreads among the people, antiquated customs and prejudices will by and by be shed, as naturally and inevitably as bud scales are shed in spring when the leaves and flowers expand in the sunshine.[2]

It may interest the reader to note that Esslemont wrote these words prior to 1923.

Robert Stockman, currently Director of the Research Office of the Bahá'í National Center of the United States, further compares and contrasts the Gandhian and the Bahá'í approaches:

Gandhi's thought on this subject was perhaps the highest and finest the world has currently produced outside the Faith. Civil disobedience, as a mechanism for social change, was impossible more than a century or so ago because it is dependent on a free press, public opinion, the rule of law, and transparency in civil proceedings. Eight hundred years ago, civil disobedience would not have worked against Genjis Khan; he would have massacred anyone like Gandhi and no one would have known. It worked against the British because they thought of themselves as a just people. Interestingly, it never worked against the French, who had to be driven violently out of Vietnam and Algeria (with consequences for both nations that continue to this day).

The Bahá'í position—which I think one could basically call "nonviolent civil obedience"—may still be as premature in this society as non-violent civil disobedience was at the time of Genjis Khan. The Bahá'í position depends on consultation as a central cultural value of society, and it isn't yet. Saying this, I think, would allow one to put the Bahá'í and Gandhian positions, which are contradictory on the surface, in a greater context.[3]

11.2   Consultation

Gandhi advocates the resolution of problems through consultation:

> Let all people sit together and find a proper solution to problems on which there are differences.[4]

Most Bahá'ís agree wholeheartedly with Gandhi's statement. Indeed, consultation plays a central role in Bahá'í political thinking. Bahá'u'lláh reconceptualizes many aspects of human relationships:

> In all things it is necessary to consult...
>
> The maturity of the gift of understanding is made manifest through consultation.[5]

Consultation is so important to the Bahá'ís that it is explained in *The Prosperity of Humankind:*[5]

> What Bahá'u'lláh is calling for is a consultative process in which the individual participants strive to transcend their respective points of view, in order to function as members of a body with its own interests and goals. In such an atmosphere, characterized by both candor and courtesy, ideas belong not to the individual to whom they occur during the discussion but to the group as a whole, to take up, discard, or revise as seems to best serve the goal pursued. Consultation succeeds to the extent that all participants support the decisions arrived at, regardless of the individual opinions with which they entered the discussion. Under such circumstances an earlier decision can be readily reconsidered if experience exposes any shortcomings.
>
> Viewed in such a light, consultation is the operating expression of justice in human affairs. So vital is it to the success of collective endeavor that it must constitute a basic feature of a viable strategy of social and economic

development. Indeed, the participation of the people on whose commitment and efforts the success of such a strategy depends becomes effective only as consultation is made the organizing principle of every project. "No man can attain his true station," is Bahá'u'lláh's counsel, "except through his justice. No power can exist except through unity. No welfare and no well-being can be attained except through consultation."[5]

11.3 Party Politics

It is perhaps obvious to the reader that party politics is intrinsically, irremediably, and devastatingly antithetical to the consultative process. (Sadly, some career politicians seem not to be able to understand that partisanship is divisive.) Party politics incorrectly assumes that humankind is not a single organism, but rather that it is divided into separate "parties." Hence, party politics can have no place in a truly nonviolent civilization built around the principles of the oneness of humankind and of consultation. The Bahá'í position is clearly explained in *The Prosperity of Humankind*:

> The standard of truth seeking [that the consultative] process demands is far beyond the patterns of negotiation and compromise that tend to characterize the present-day discussion of human affairs. It cannot be achieved—indeed, its attainment is severely handicapped—by the culture of protest that is another widely prevailing feature of contemporary society. Debate, propaganda, the adversarial method, the entire apparatus of partisanship that have long been such familiar features of collective action are all fundamentally harmful to its purpose: that is, arriving at a consensus about the truth of a given situation and the wisest choice of action among the options open at any given moment.

Indeed, the principles of the oneness of humankind and of consultation are so important to the Bahá'ís that they are strictly prohibited from affiliating with political parties.

Gandhi also realized this point and towards the end of his life increasingly withdrew from party politics for reasons similar to those given above. Gandhi, like the Bahá'ís, felt that party politics is fundamentally based on disunity:

> ... our greatest defect is that, as soon as we differ from somebody ever so slightly, or a misunderstanding arises, instead of meeting the person concerned and trying to find a solution we take him to task publicly. This creates a great mental gulf between people, leading to antagonism. Parties and isms are only results of such differences.

Today, the democratic process by which we elect members of parliaments and other collective bodies is deeply mired and entrenched in fallacies regarding the hypothetical need for nominations, candidature, electioneering, and solicitation. As our species becomes progressively educated, however, we will be able to adopt electoral procedures that will "clean" our political process. If readers entertain any doubts regarding the feasibility of conducting elections without going through electioneering, etc., then they stand to benefit from an impartial study of the Bahá'í model. The several million strong worldwide Bahá'í community elects their representatives yearly at the local and national levels. Election meetings typically begin with prayers. All adult Bahá'ís belonging to their local or national community (respectively) and in good standing are eligible, but those who engage in electioneering or partisan activities risk being disqualified. Under present guidelines, the nine people who receive the largest number of votes are elected to the local or national institution, respectively. At the international level, the elections for the membership of the Universal House of Justice are held every five years instead of yearly, but otherwise the process is similar.[6] Since the Bahá'í election process strictly prohibits electioneering, therefore the elected Bahá'í "Assemblies" enjoy a climate in which the perennial tendencies toward manipulation and partisanship are far less likely to deflect the decision-making process. Unless other communities and institutions adopt measures similar to those used by Bahá'ís, it is impossible to envision how the democratic culture will be able to rid itself of the cynicism, apathy, and corruption to which party politics has given rise.

11.4 Village Autonomy

The importance of decentralized power structures has already been discussed in Section 5.4. Indeed, limited village autonomy is a common theme in Bahá'í and Gandhian thinking. Esslemont writes:

> 'Abdu'l-Bahá suggests that each town and village or district should be entrusted as far as possible with the administration of fiscal matters within its own area and should contribute its due proportion for the expenses of the general government. One of the principal sources of revenue should be a graduated income tax. If a man's income does not exceed his necessary expenditure he should not be required to pay any tax, but in all cases where income exceeds the necessary expenditure a tax should be levied, the percentage of tax increasing as the surplus of income over necessary expenditure increases. On the other hand, if a person, through illness, poor crops, or other cause for which he is not responsible, is unable to earn an income sufficient to meet his necessary expenses for the year, then what he lacks for the maintenance of himself and his family should be supplied out of public funds. There will also be other sources of public revenue, e.g. from intestate estates, mines, treasure trove and voluntary contributions; while among the expenditures will be grants for the support of the infirm, of orphans, of schools, of the deaf and blind, and for the maintenance of public health. Thus the welfare and comfort of all will be provided for.[7]

Similarly, Gandhi writes:

> My idea of village *swaraj* [self-rule] is that it is a complete republic, independent of its neighbors for its own vital wants, and yet interdependent for many others in

which dependence is a necessity. Thus every village's
first concern will be to grow its own food crops and
cotton for its cloth. It should have a reserve for its
cattle, recreation and playground for adults and children. Then if there is more land available, it will grow
useful money crops, thus excluding *ganja* [made from
cannabis plants], tobacco, opium and the like. The village will maintain a village theatre, school and public
hall. It will have its own waterworks, ensuring clean
water supply. This can be done through controlled
wells or tanks. Education will be compulsory up to
the final basic course. As far as possible every activity
will be conducted on the co-operative basis...

The government of the village will be conducted by
a Panchayat of five persons annually elected by the
adult villagers, male and female, possessing the minimum prescribed qualifications.[8]

It is interesting to compare Gandhi's description of the Panchayat
with local Bahá'í Spiritual Assemblies. The latter comprise nine
persons, elected annually by each local Bahá'í community, in which
is vested the authority of decision on all matters of mutual action
on the part of the community. This designation is temporary, since
in the future these Spiritual Assemblies will be termed Houses of
Justice. A full discussion about Bahá'í administration[6] is well
beyond the scope of this book.

11.5   Development

An essential feature of decentralized politics is that the arena of
social and economic transformation no longer remains the exclusive privilege of career politicians: every adult human being can
participate in social and economic development activities. In fact,
politicians never did have such a monopoly.

There is no doubt that social and economic development activities have to offer very significant contributions towards the goal
of a nonviolent civilization. Gandhi's attempt at social and economic development of villages, as outlined in his *Constructive Pro*

gramme,[9] has a number of features in common with Bahá'í social
and economic development projects, of which there were over 1 700
in number during 1996–1997.[10] Much has been written about the
Constructive Programme, and there is also quite a large body of
Bahá'í literature on the subject of development. Three principles Gandhi and the Bahá'ís appear to have in common are worth
mentioning: (i) reliance on grass roots implementation and driving
forces, (ii) a balanced approach involving spiritual as well as practical dimensions of development, and (iii) an emphasis on selfless
service to humankind.

The subject of social and economic development is too large a
topic for further consideration in this book (see also the index).

11.6 A Paralysis of Will

Unfortunately, many people in the past and even today believe
that human nature is irremedially selfish. This dogma does not
correspond to any scientifically established truth. Yet, people have
clung to it and thereby forfeited fantastic opportunities that could
have been seized. One reason why people have tended to think in
this way is due to the commonly known fact that change can be
extremely slow. For example, it can take decades and centuries
for a tree to grow and give fruit. Similarly, it has taken millions
of years for humans to evolve. Nevertheless, to think that human
nature cannot improve is an extremely flawed conclusion. Gandhi
writes:

> We do see men constantly becoming better under effort
> and discipline. There is no occasion for limiting the
> capacity for improvement. Life to me would lose all its
> interest if I felt that I could not attain perfect love on
> earth. After all, what matters, is that our capacity for
> loving ever expands...[11]

Bahá'ís believe that it is essential for us to reject the idea that we
cannot grow and improve through effort. The Universal House of
Justice*, in *The Promise of World Peace* explains:

---

*The supreme ruling body of the Bahá'ís. See Chapter 1.

Indeed, so much have aggression and conflict come to characterize our social, economic and religious systems, that many have succumbed to the view that such behaviour is intrinsic to human nature and therefore ineradicable.

With the entrenchment of this view, a paralyzing contradiction has developed in human affairs. On the one hand, people of all nations proclaim not only their readiness but their longing for peace and harmony, for an end to the harrowing apprehensions tormenting their daily lives. On the other, uncritical assent is given to the proposition that human beings are incorrigibly selfish and aggressive and thus incapable of erecting a social system at once progressive and peaceful, dynamic and harmonious, a system giving free play to individual creativity and initiative but based on co-operation and reciprocity.

As the need for peace becomes more urgent, this fundamental contradiction, which hinders its realization, demands a reassessment of the assumptions upon which the commonly held view of mankind's historical predicament is based. Dispassionately examined, the evidence reveals that such conduct, far from expressing man's true self, represents a distortion of the human spirit. Satisfaction on this point will enable all people to set in motion constructive social forces which, because they are consistent with human nature, will encourage harmony and co-operation instead of war and conflict.[12]

Esslemont also touches on some of these points:

Education and religion are alike based on the assumption that it is possible to change human nature. In fact, it requires but little investigation to show that the one thing we can say with certainty about any living thing is that it cannot keep from changing. Without change there can be no life. Even the mineral cannot

resist change, and the higher we go in the scale of being, the more varied, complex, and wonderful do the
changes become. Moreover, in progress and development among creatures of all grades we find two kinds
of change—one slow, gradual, often almost impercep-
tible; and the other rapid, sudden and dramatic. The
latter occur at what are called "critical stages" of development. In the case of minerals we find such critical
stages at the melting and boiling points, for example,
when the solid suddenly becomes a liquid or the liquid
becomes a gas. In the case of plants we see such critical
stages when the seed begins to germinate, or the bud
bursts into leaf. In the animal world we see the same
on every hand, as when the grub suddenly changes into
a butterfly, the chick emerges from its shell, or the babe
is born from its mother's womb.

In the higher life of the soul we often see a similar transformation, when a man is "born again" and his whole
being becomes radically changed in its aims, its character and activities. Such critical stages often affect a
whole species or multitude of species simultaneously, as
when vegetation of all kinds suddenly bursts into new
life in springtime.

Bahá'u'lláh declares that just as lesser living things
have times of sudden emergence into new and fuller
life, so for mankind also a "critical stage," a time of
"rebirth," is at hand. Then modes of life which have
persisted from the dawn of history up till now will be
quickly, irrevocably, altered, and humanity [will] enter
on a new phase of life as different from the old as the
butterfly is different from the caterpillar, or the bird
from the egg. Mankind as a whole, in the light of new
Revelation, will attain to a new vision of truth; as a
whole country is illumined when the sun rises, so that
all men see clearly, where but an hour before everything
was dark and dim. "This is a new cycle of human
power," says 'Abdu'l-Bahá. "All the horizons of the

world are luminous, and the world will become indeed
as a rose garden and a paradise." The analogies of nature are all in favor of such a view; the Prophets of old
have with one accord foretold the advent of such a glorious day; the signs of the times show clearly that profound and revolutionary changes in human ideas and
institutions are even now in progress. What could be
more futile and baseless therefore, than the pessimistic
argument that, although all things else change, human
nature cannot change?[13]

11.7   A New Paradigm

It may interest the reader to note that Esslemont's use above of
the idea of "criticality" predates the rise of the field of *critical phenomena* in the academic study of statistical physics. His use of the
word "complex" similarly prefigures the widespread use of terms
like "complexity" and "complex systems." If the simple physics
of the pendulum inspired the contemporary democratic culture of
bipolar partisan politics, then perhaps it is not inconceivable that
the new physics of complex systems and cooperative and critical
phenomena will herald a new political culture. Is there not a better
model to follow than the pendulum? Indeed, such a model does
exist.

There is one complex system that is mentioned by both Gandhi
as well as in the Bahá'í writings that can serve as a better model—
or paradigm—for politics: the organism of the human body*. According to this model, the body of humankind is a single organism, much like the physical human body. This analogy captures
the fundamental principle of the oneness of humankind (as applied
to politics and economics), but it also projects a spiritual dimension that is altogether absent for the pendulum: the human body
is a "temple" where mind meets matter, heaven illumines earth,
and spirit enters flesh. This model is compatible with both the
organic as well as the spiritual characteristics of humankind. The
adoption of this model of politics, and of human affairs in general,

---

*See also Section 6.2.

will at once create the conditions needed to resolve outstanding social, economic, and political problems for which no solution can be found in the old party-political framework.

Chapter Notes

1. *The Essential Writings of Mahatma Gandhi.* Ed. Raghavan Iyer (Oxford: Oxford University Press, 1990), 335.

2. J. E. Esslemont, *Bahá'u'lláh and the New Era,* 5th rev. ed. (Wilmette: Bahá'í Publishing Trust, 1987), 149–150.

3. Robert Stockman, personal communication (E-mail), 9 September 1998.

4. *The Essential Writings of Mahatma Gandhi,* 361.

5. *The Prosperity Of Humankind,* A statement prepared by the Bahá'í International Community's Office of Public Information.

6. See, for example, Shoghi Effendi, *Bahá'í Administration* (Wilmette: Bahá'í Publishing Trust, 1974).

7. *Bahá'u'lláh and the New Era,* 141–142.

8. *The Essential Writings of Mahatma Gandhi,* 358–359.

9. See, for example, *Constructive Programme: Its Meaning and Place,* which may be found in *The Selected Works of Mahatma Gandhi: Volume Four (the Basic Works).* Ed. Shriman Narayan (Ahmedabad: Navajivan Publishing House, 1968), 187.

10. *Bahá'í Social and Economic Development Activities: 1996–1997,* Prepared by the Office of Social and Economic Development, Bahá'í World Centre.

11. *The Essential Writings of Mahatma Gandhi,* 167.

12. *The Promise of World Peace.* A statement of the Universal House of Justice addressed to the peoples of the world, dated October 1985.

13. *Bahá'u'lláh and the New Era,* 118–119.

Chapter 12

Vegetarianism

As we collectively embark upon the building of a nonviolent civilization, it is prudent to take a closer look at the assumptions and values that underlie our diets. There are a number of potential advantages in vegetarian and vegan* diets. While the discussion of vegetarianism has in the past been centered around health and the treatment of animals, there is also an important environmental aspect that only recently has received serious attention. It is an established fact that, on average, it takes a significantly larger area of land to grow food for a meat-eating individual than for a vegetarian person. Hence, if most of the world opted for a vegetarian diet, it would be significantly less taxing on our environment.

It should be stressed that vegetarianism is not considered a major issue in the Bahá'í community. Indeed, Bahá'ís are not generally vegetarian, coming as they do from every part of the earth and from many religious and ethnic backgrounds. However, many Bahá'í teachings on diet are similar to those of Gandhi, an ardent vegetarian.

While there are no dietary restrictions in the Bahá'í Faith (aside from the prohibition against intoxicants), Shoghi Effendi said, "It is certain, however, that if man can live on a purely vegetarian diet and thus avoid killing animals, it would be much preferable."[1] Furthermore, 'Abdu'l-Bahá said, "Fruits and grains [will be the

---

*Vegans eat no animal meat, no milk, no eggs.

foods of the future]. The time will come when meat will no longer
be eaten. Medical science is only in its infancy, yet it has shown
that our natural diet is that which grows out of the ground."[2]
It should be noted that many Bahá'ís all over the world opt for
vegetarian diets and even Bahá'ís from traditionally meat-eating
cultures are slowly becoming vegetarian.

12.1   Vegetarian Foods Best

Gandhi felt that a vegetarian diet is best suited to the human
digestive system:

> Medical opinion is mostly in favour of a mixed [non-
> vegetarian] diet, although there is a growing school,
> which is strongly of the opinion that anatomical and
> physiological evidence is in favour of man being a vege-
> tarian. His teeth, his stomach, intestines, etc., seem to
> prove that nature has meant man to be a vegetarian.[3]

The Bahá'í Faith similarly teaches that humans are not really
meant to eat animals. 'Abdu'l-Bahá writes,

> Regarding the eating of animal flesh and abstinence
> therefrom, know thou of a certainty that, in the be-
> ginning of creation, God determined the food of every
> living being, and to eat contrary to that determination
> is not approved. For instance, beasts of prey, such as
> the wolf, lion, and leopard, are endowed with ferocious,
> tearing instruments, such as hooked talons and claws.
> From this it is evident that the food of such beasts is
> meat. If they were to attempt to graze, their teeth
> would not cut the grass, neither could they chew the
> cud, for they do not have molars. Likewise, God hath
> given to the four-footed grazing animals such teeth as
> reap the grass like a sickle, and from this we understand
> that the food of these species of animal is vegetable.
> They cannot chase and hunt down other animals. The
> falcon hath a hooked beak and sharp talons; the hooked

beak preventeth him from grazing, therefore his food is also meat.

But now coming to man, we see he hath neither hooked teeth nor sharp nails or claws, nor teeth like iron sickles. From this it becometh evident and manifest that the food of man is cereals and fruit. Some of the teeth of man are like millstones to grind the grain, and some are sharp to cut the fruit. Therefore he is not in need of meat, nor is he obliged to eat it. Even without eating meat he would live with the utmost vigour and energy. For example, the community of the Brahmins in India do not eat meat; notwithstanding this they are not inferior to other nations in strength, power, vigour, outward senses or intellectual virtues.[4]

As humanity progresses, meat will be used less and less, for the teeth of man are not carnivorous. For example, the lion is endowed with carnivorous teeth, which are intended for meat, and if meat be not found, the lion starves. The lion cannot graze; its teeth are of different shape. The digestive system of the lion is such that it cannot receive nourishment save through meat. The eagle has a crooked beak, the lower part shorter than the upper. It cannot pick up grain; it cannot graze; therefore, it is compelled to partake of meat. The domestic animals have herbivorous teeth formed to cut grass, which is their fodder. The human teeth, the molars, are formed to grind grain. The front teeth, the incisors, are for fruits, etc. It is, therefore, quite apparent according to the implements for eating that man's food is intended to be grain and not meat. When mankind is more fully developed, the eating of meat will gradually cease.[5]

12.2 Vegetarianism and Nonviolence

Both Gandhi and 'Abdu'l-Bahá felt that the killing of animals for food is somewhat contrary to nonviolence and compassion, and suggested alternatives to meat. 'Abdu'l-Bahá writes,

> Truly, the killing of animals and the eating of their
> meat is somewhat contrary to pity and compassion,
> and if one can content oneself with cereals, fruit, oil
> and nuts, such as pistachios, almonds and so on, it
> would undoubtedly be better and more pleasing.[4]

Gandhi writes,

> I do feel that spiritual progress does demand at some
> stage that we should cease to kill our fellow-creatures
> for the satisfaction of our bodily wants.[6]

> Vegetarian diet, besides grains, pulses, edible roots, tu-
> bers and leaves, includes fruits, both fresh and dry.
> Dry fruit includes nuts like almonds, pistachios, wal-
> nut, etc.[3]

While both Gandhi and the Bahá'ís agree that the killing of
animals for food may be somewhat immoral, they both emphasize
the importance of not blowing the issue out of proportion. Gandhi
writes,

> It is wrong to over-estimate the importance of food in
> the formation of character or in subjugating the flesh.
> Diet is a powerful factor not to be neglected. But to
> sum up all religion in terms of diet, as is often done in
> India, is as wrong as it is to disregard all restraint in
> regard to diet and to give full reins to one's appetite.[7]

Perhaps for this same reason, vegetarianism has not been made a
central teaching of the Bahá'í Faith, even though it is very much
encouraged.

12.3   Kindness to Animals

'Abdu'l-Bahá and Gandhi both felt that our stewardship of animals
and our relationships with other life forms should be governed by
mercy and kindness towards them. 'Abdu'l-Bahá writes regarding
the treatment of animals,

Briefly, it is not only their fellow human beings that the beloved of God must treat with mercy and compassion, rather must they show forth the utmost loving-kindness to every living creature. For in all physical respects, and where the animal spirit is concerned, the selfsame feelings are shared by animal and man. Man hath not grasped this truth, however, and he believeth that physical sensations are confined to human beings, wherefore is he unjust to the animals, and cruel.

And yet in truth, what difference is there when it cometh to physical sensations? The feelings are one and the same, whether ye inflict pain on man or on beast. There is no difference here whatever. And indeed ye do worse to harm an animal, for man hath a language, he can lodge a complaint, he can cry out and moan; if injured he can have recourse to the authorities and these will protect him from his aggressor. But the hapless beast is mute, able neither to express its hurt nor take its case to the authorities. If a man inflict a thousand ills upon a beast, it can neither ward him off with speech nor hale him into court. Therefore is it essential that ye show forth the utmost consideration to the animal, and that ye be even kinder to him than to your fellow man.

Train your children from their earliest days to be infinitely tender and loving to animals. If an animal be sick, let the children try to heal it, if it be hungry, let them feed it, if thirsty, let them quench its thirst, if weary, let them see that it rests.

Most human beings are sinners, but the beasts are innocent. Surely those without sin should receive the most kindness and love—all except animals which are harmful, such as bloodthirsty wolves, such as poisonous snakes, and similar pernicious creatures, the reason being that kindness to these is an injustice to human beings and to other animals as well. If, for example, ye be tender-hearted toward a wolf, this is but tyranny to a

sheep, for a wolf will destroy a whole flock of sheep. A
rabid dog, if given the chance, can kill a thousand animals and men. Therefore, compassion shown to wild
and ravening beasts is cruelty to the peaceful ones—
and so the harmful must be dealt with. But to blessed
animals the utmost kindness must be shown, the more
the better. Tenderness and loving-kindness are basic
principles of God's heavenly Kingdom. Ye should most
carefully bear this matter in mind.[8]

The above passage raises an interesting point: in order to exercise kindness towards humans or other creatures, it may become
necessary to kill or harm other creatures. Gandhi also recognized
this fact:

In life it is impossible to eschew violence completely.
The question arises, where is one to draw the line? The
line cannot be the same for everyone. Although essentially the principle is the same, yet everyone applies it
in his or her own way. What is one man's food can
be another man's poison. Meat-eating is a sin for me.
Yet, for another person, who has always lived on meat
and never seen anything wrong, to give it up simply in
order to copy me will be a sin.

If I wish to be an agriculturist and stay in the jungle, I
will have to use the minimum unavoidable violence in
order to protect my fields. I will have to kill monkeys,
birds, and insects which eat up my crops... To allow
crops to be eaten up by animals in the name of Ahimsa
while there is a famine in the land is certainly a sin.
Evil and good are relative terms. What is good under
certain conditions can become an evil or a sin under a
different set of conditions.[9]

12.4 Holistic Considerations

A comprehensive look at vegetarianism—one which takes into account issues such as ecological sustainability and dietary health—is

beyond the scope of this book. However, the overall picture that emerges from the Bahá'í holy scriptures and from Gandhi's teachings is that a vegetarian diet, wherever possible to practice, is better in most ways to a diet which includes animal meat.

Chapter Notes

1. Shoghi Effendi, quoted in *Lights of Guidance: A Bahá'í Reference File,* 2nd Edition. Ed. Helen Hornby (New Delhi: Bahá'í Publishing Trust, 1988), 296.

2. J. E. Esslemont, *Bahá'u'lláh and the New Era,* 5th rev. ed. (Wilmette: Bahá'í Publishing Trust, 1987), 102.

3. *The Selected Works of Mahatma Gandhi: Volume Four (the Basic Works).* Ed. Shriman Narayan (Ahmedabad: Navajivan Publishing House, 1968), 407.

4. 'Abdu'l-Bahá, quoted in *Lights of Guidance; A Bahai Reference File,* 295.

5. *The Promulgation of Universal Peace: Talks Delivered by 'Abdu'l-Bahá during His Visit to the United States and Canada in 1912* (Wilmette: Bahá'í Publishing Trust, 1982), 170–1.

6. *The Mind of Mahatma Gandhi.* Ed. R. K. Prabhu and U. R. Rao (Ahmedabad: Navajivan Publishing House, 1967), 466.

7. *The Mind of Mahatma Gandhi,* 464.

8. *Selections from the Writings of 'Abdu'l-Bahá* (Haifa: Bahá'í World Centre, 1978), 159–60.

9. M. K. Gandhi, *In Search of the Supreme. Volume Three.* Ed. V. B. Kher (Ahmedabad: Navajivan press, 1962), 207.

Chapter 13

Major Differences

The previous chapters may have left the reader with the impression
that Gandhi and the Bahá'ís agree on practically everything, so
this chapter examines important differences.

13.1   Truth versus Unity

Gandhi's fundamental principles are truth and nonviolence. In
contrast, it can be argued that the fundamental principle of the
Bahá'í Faith is unity. Hence, it should not come as a surprise if
Gandhi and the Bahá'ís assign different priorities to these principles.

For instance, Gandhi did consent to become the cause of disunity in order not to compromise on the principle truth. Indeed,
Gandhi believed that it is more important to be correct and truth-
ful than to be united. This philosophical approach is a natural
consequence of Gandhi's belief that Truth is God. A classic example of Gandhi's emphasis on truth—to the point of compromising
on the principle of unity—is his attitude towards unjust and tyrannical governments.* Indeed, Gandhi believed it was a wrong *not*
to oppose (nonviolently) an unjust government. In contrast, the
Bahá'ís believe that it is more important to be united than to be
correct. Essentially, Gandhi believed that Truth is higher than

---
*See also Section.11.1.

Unity, while Bahá'ís believe that Unity is more important than
Truth. 'Abdu'l-Bahá explains:

> It is my hope that the friends... become united on all
> subjects and not disagree at all. If they agree upon a
> subject, even though it be wrong, it is better than to
> disagree and be in the right, for this difference will pro-
> duce the demolition of the divine foundation. Though
> one of the parties may be in the right and they disagree
> that will be the cause of a thousand wrongs, but if they
> agree and both parties are in the wrong, as it is in unity
> the truth will be revealed and the wrong made right.[1]

13.2   Disobedience to Government

One logical consequence of the different priorities Gandhi and the
Bahá'ís assign to the principles of Truth and of Unity is their difference of approach towards obedience to government. Gandhi
believed that it is correct and moral to disobey an unjust government, so long as it is done nonviolently. In contrast, Bahá'ís believe
that the government should be obeyed always, except where such
obedience would be directly against Bahá'í ethics and laws.[*]

13.3   Progressive Revelation

Gandhi believed that all religions are equal and that therefore there
is no need for a person to change their declared religion.[†] According to Gandhi, it is sufficient if all people study each other's
religions.   There is no need to "convert," because all religions
mirror Truth. In contrast, although Bahá'ís do believe that all·the
religions are equally divine in origin and purpose, they also believe
that each religion has its appropriate time and place in history.
For example, it would be a great step backward for humankind to
return to the days of ritual animal sacrifices. Similarly, the age-old
customs of caste-based divisions have now been superseded by the

---

[*]See also section 11.1.
[†]See also Section 3.5.

principle of the oneness of humankind.* As a child grows, its needs change—likewise is it with humankind. Bahá'ís believe that since Religion is progressive and revolutionary in nature, therefore no single religious system can last forever. Hence, religions supersede one another as the times change—even the Bahá'í Faith will, in a distant future, be superseded by a new religion. Religious conversion, far from being avoidable, is a necessity according to the Bahá'ís. If early Hindus had not converted to the "new" faith of Lord Buddha and if Jews had not converted to the new Faith of Jesus Christ, then Buddhism and Christianity would never have spread.† The very first duty of a person, according to the Kitáb-i-Aqdas, is recognition of the Manifestation of God for the age in which one lives. Essentially, Gandhi did not believe in what Bahá'ís call progressive revelation.

Of course, Bahá'ís completely agree with Gandhi that people should never be forced to convert. Proselytization—i.e., religious conversion of one person by another—is strictly forbidden in the Bahá'í Faith. Rather, people must have absolute freedom of choice in purely personal matters of faith.

13.4 Sexuality

Gandhi believed that sexual intercourse is intended only for reproduction. He believed that enjoying sexual pleasures is a sin. Gandhi said to Margaret Sanger, leader of the planned parenthood movement in America,

> If they [the married couple] do not want to have children, they should simply refuse to unite [in sexual intercourse].[2]

Gandhi even believed that sin is proportional to pleasure! In contrast, Bahá'ís believe that it is healthy to enjoy the pleasures of married life. Absolute chastity before marriage, and complete faithfulness to the spouse after marriage characterize the ideal Bahá'í marriage. Shoghi Effendi explains:

---

*See also Section 13.7.
†See also Section 3.5.

Chastity in the strict sense means not to have sexual intercourse, or sexual intimacies, before marriage. In the general sense it means not to be licentious. This does not mean we Bahá'ís believe sexual relations to be impure or wrong. On the contrary they are natural and should be considered one of God's many blessings... Sex is a very individual matter, some people are more passionate by nature than others, and might consequently suffer more if forced to be continent. But when the world becomes more spiritual there will not be such an exaggerated emphasis on sex, as there is today, and consequently it will be easier for young people to be chaste and control their passions. A man of noble character and strong willpower, could certainly remain faithful to his wife during a long absence![3]

In Gandhi's days, science had not yet advanced to the point where human reproduction and sexuality were properly understood. It is now well known that human sexual behavior plays important reproductive roles besides the obvious function it has in fertilization and conception. For example, sex is important for "pair bonding." Such bonding between the male and female parents is essential—without it a child will likely be raised in a "single parent" home. There is growing evidence that single parenting, though perfectly fine for raising kittens, puppies, etc., is not good for raising children. Unlike our primate cousins whose infants mature very quickly, human infants require some 15 years to mature fully. This is why humans are unsuited to the polygamous, promiscuous reproductive strategy used by our primate cousins, and more suited instead to the formation of (more or less) stable monogamous pairs of male and female. Indeed, sexuality plays a central role in keeping human couples together, at least initially. Since Gandhi thought that sex was fine for reproduction, perhaps he would have taken a less puritanical stance on sex had he known what we know today about the biological, psychological, and sociological aspects of human sexuality. It is fascinating to note that Gandhi seems to have tolerated the so-called "natural" birth control methods, which are inherently nonviolent. (It can conceivably be argued that hormone pills, IUDs, spermicides, etc.

are slightly "violent" forms of contraception that can harm the body.) Mahadev Desai, who was present when Gandhi met Mrs. Sanger, writes:

> ... Gandhiji did mention a remedy which could conceivably appeal to him. That method was the avoidance of sexual union during unsafe periods, confining it to the "safe" period of about ten days during the month. That had at least an element of self-control which had to be exercised during the unsafe period. Whether this appealed to Mrs. Sanger or not I do not know.[4]

13.5 Interpretation of Scripture

On many issues, Gandhi's approach to interpretation of sacred scripture is consistent with the approach found in the Bahá'í Faith,* but there are exceptions. Gandhi usually interpreted scripture more or less literally. For example, he interpreted the Sermon on the Mount more literally than did many contemporary Christian theologians. Such a literal approach to interpretation is fine in many cases. But every now and then, Gandhi runs into problems because no literal interpretation appears possible in some cases.

Consider the following illustrative example. Gandhi translates verses 24–26 of Book VIII of the *Gita,* which concern the conditions that determine the exemption from "return" of souls after death, as follows:

> 24.   Fire, Light, Day, the Bright Fortnight, the six months of the Northern Solstice—through these departing men knowing *Brahman* go to *Brahman.*

> 25 Smoke, Night, the Dark Fortnight, the six months of the Southern Solstice—therethrough the *yogin* attains to the lunar light and thence returns.

> 26. These two paths—bright and dark—are deemed to be the eternal paths of the world; by the one a man goes to return not, by the other he returns again.[5]

---

*See also Chapter 3.

These admittedly esoteric verses suggest that a person can attain *moksha, nirvana,* or salvation merely by dying in the correct season or time period. Gandhi confesses his difficulty in applying such a literal approach to the interpretation of the first two verses, and himself attempts a metaphorical approach to their interpretation:

> I do not understand the meaning of these two *shlokas* [verses 24–25]. They do not seem to me to be consistent with the teaching of the Gita. The Gita teaches that he whose heart is meek with devotion, who is devoted to unattached action and has seen the Truth must win salvation, no matter when he dies. These *shlokas* seem to run counter to this. They may perhaps be stretched to mean broadly that a man of sacrifice, a man of light, a man who has known *Brahman* [God] finds release from birth if he retains that enlightenment at the time of death, and that on the contrary the man who has none of these attributes goes to the world of the moon—not at all lasting—and returns to birth. The moon, after all, shines with borrowed light![5]

Gandhi, like most Bahá'ís, finds it difficult to believe the incredible proposition that the positions of the sun and the moon in the sky can dictate whether a person will find liberation! Gandhi's interpretation, which he modestly describes as "stretched," is far more acceptable to most Bahá'ís than the literal one. Bahá'u'lláh explains that sacred scripture has multiple levels of meaning. Sometimes the intended meaning is literal, but at other times the meaning is "hidden" and can only be properly understood through metaphorical or allegorical interpretation. This idea can also be found in the parables of Jesus Christ, such as when he said "let the dead bury their dead." Obviously, a dead person cannot bury another dead person, rather Jesus was referring to people who are "spiritually dead." In the aptly titled Kitáb-i-Íqán (the Book of Certitude), written more than 15 years before Gandhi was born, Bahá'u'lláh explains that the best way to interpret scripture is the one that takes us closest to the Truth:

> It is evident unto thee that the Birds of Heaven and Doves of Eternity speak a twofold language. One lan-

guage, the outward language, is devoid of allusions, is
unconcealed and unveiled; that it may be a guiding
lamp and a beaconing light whereby wayfarers may attain the heights of holiness, and seekers may advance
into the realm of eternal reunion... The other language is veiled and concealed, so that whatever lieth
hidden in the heart of the malevolent may be made
manifest and their innermost being be disclosed...
This is the divine standard, this is the Touchstone
of God, wherewith He proveth His servants. None
apprehendeth the meaning of these utterances except
them whose hearts are assured, whose souls have found
favour with God, and whose minds are detached from
all else but Him. In such utterances the literal meaning, as generally understood by the people, is not what
hath been intended... [6]

Moreover, in the Kitáb-i-Íqán, Bahá'u'lláh specifically explains
that the terms sun and moon, found in sacred scripture, can be
used as metaphors, and counsels readers to renounce attachment
to the letter of sacred scripture, that they may thereby attain to
its spirit:

By the terms "sun" and "moon," mentioned in the
writings of the Prophets of God, is not meant solely
the sun and moon of the visible universe. Nay rather,
manifold are the meanings they have intended for these
terms. In every instance they have attached to them
a particular significance. Thus, by the "sun" in one
sense is meant those Suns of Truth Who rise from the
dayspring of ancient glory, and fill the world with a
liberal effusion of grace from on high. These Suns of
Truth are the universal Manifestations of God in the
worlds of His attributes and names...

In another sense, by these terms is intended the divines
of the former Dispensation, who live in the days of
the subsequent Revelations, and who hold the reins of
religion in their grasp...

In another sense, by the terms 'sun', 'moon', and 'stars'

are meant such laws and teachings as have been established and proclaimed in every Dispensation, such as
the laws of prayer and fasting...

O my brother! Take thou the step of the spirit, so
that, swift as the twinkling of an eye, thou mayest flash
through the wilds of remoteness and bereavement, attain the Riḍván [paradise] of everlasting reunion, and
in one breath commune with the heavenly Spirits. For
with human feet thou canst never hope to traverse these
immeasurable distances, nor attain thy goal. Peace
be upon him whom the light of truth guideth unto all
truth, and who, in the name of God, standeth in the
path of His Cause, upon the shore of true understanding.[7]

According to this point of view, Gandhi was entirely justified in
his attempt to "stretch" the meaning of *Gita 8:24–25.* Indeed,
the literal meaning is not what Krishna most probably intended.
Gandhi's comment on verse 26, about the bright and dark paths of
the world, further shows that he was not against using metaphors
in interpretation:

The Bright one may be taken to mean the path of
knowledge and the dark one that of ignorance.[8]

Hence, although far from being identical, Gandhi's approach to
interpretation is not altogether inconsistent with the Bahá'í approach.* Further evidence of Gandhi's flexibility towards interpretation is his willingness to regard the *Mahabharata* not as a literal
history but as a mythic one:

Even in 1888–89, when I first became acquainted with
the *Gita,* I felt that it was not a historical work, but
that, under the guise of physical warfare, it described
the duel that perpetually went on in the hearts of
mankind, and that physical warfare was brought in
merely to make the description of the internal duel
more alluring. This preliminary intuition became more

---

*See also Chapter 3.

confirmed on a closer study of religion and the *Gita*. A
study of the *Mahabharata* gave it added confirmation.
I do not regard the *Mahabharata* as a historical work
in the accepted sense. The *Adiparva** contains powerful evidence in support of my opinion. By ascribing to
the chief actors superhuman or subhuman origins, the
great Vyasa made short work of the history of kings
and their peoples. The persons therein described may
be historical, but the author of the *Mahabharata* has
used them merely to drive home his religious theme.[9]

13.6 Reincarnation and Death

A classic example where Gandhi and the Bahá'ís differ in their
interpretations of sacred scripture relates to the subject of reincarnation. The sacred scriptures of the Hindu and Buddhist faiths
mention reincarnation of the soul, and state that when a person
dies, their karma dictates to a large extent the circumstances sur-
rounding their next birth. After a number of births and deaths,
the soul eventually attains its final "release." (In contrast, Christians, Muslims, and many others believe that after death they will
be judged and finally end up either in hell or in heaven.)

Bahá'ís do not believe in reincarnation, but Gandhi appears
to have believed in the traditional Hindu idea of reincarnation.
Specifically, Bahá'ís do not believe that the soul of a dead person
is reborn again on earth to live a new life. Nor, for that matter, do
they believe in a literal ("geographical") heaven or a literal hell.
Bahá'ís tend to believe that a literal approach to the interpretation of the concepts of "rebirth," "return," "heaven", "hell" etc. is
inconsistent with science, and that these ideas refer instead to essentially metaphorical—not literal—realities. Indeed, Bahá'u'lláh
has explained that terms like "hell," "heaven," "rebirth," and "return" used in the holy books of the world religions are abstractions,
metaphors, and should not be taken literally. He comments further
about such terms:

Know verily that the purpose underlying all these sym-

---

*The first book of the epic.

bolic terms and abstruse allusions, which emanate from the Revealers of God's holy Cause, hath been to test and prove the peoples of the world; that thereby the earth of the pure and illuminated hearts may be known from the perishable and barren soil. From time immemorial such hath been the way of God amidst His creatures, and to this testify the records of the sacred books...

Wert thou to cleanse the mirror of thy heart from the dust of malice, thou wouldst apprehend the meaning of the symbolic terms revealed by the all-embracing Word of God made manifest in every Dispensation, and wouldst discover the mysteries of divine knowledge. Not, however, until thou consumest with the flame of utter detachment those veils of idle learning, that are current amongst men, canst thou behold the resplendent morn of true knowledge. Know verily that Knowledge is of two kinds: Divine and Satanic. The one welleth out from the fountain of divine inspiration; the other is but a reflection of vain and obscure thoughts...

O brother, behold how the inner mysteries of "rebirth," of "return," and of "resurrection" have each... been unveiled and unravelled before thine eyes. God grant that through His gracious and invisible assistance, thou mayest divest thy body and soul of the old garment, and array thyself with the new and imperishable attire.[10]

Bahá'u'lláh originally addressed the Kitáb-i-Íqán to people versed in Muslim and Christian traditions, so the specific shades of meaning attached to metaphors such as "return" and "rebirth" are likely to be somewhat different when applied to the interpretation of these same metaphors as they occur in Hindu and Buddhist sacred scripture. But the fundamental point expressed by Bahá'u'lláh above—that concepts like "return" are metaphors—applies easily and equally to the sacred writings of all religions. For example, the word "worm" refers literally to a kind of animal. But applied to humans, the word "worm" can denote extreme baseness. So when we read in the *Kaushitaki Upanishad* that a human is "reborn here either as a worm, or as a butterfly, or as a fish, or as a bird, or as a lion, or as a serpent, or as a tiger, or as a person, or as some other being in this or in that condition, according to his works, according to his knowledge,"[11] it does not necessarily mean that the person will be literally born as a worm, etc. An interpretation far more palatable to Bahá'ís is that in the next life, the person will have the qualities we associate with worms, such as extreme baseness. The worm, butterfly, fish, bird, lion, tiger, serpent, etc. are all metaphors.

Bahá'ís completely reject reincarnation as anything besides a powerful metaphor, but they do believe that human consciousness continues to function when our physical bodies die. Since we cannot fully grasp the nature of life after death while we continue to live in this world, our understanding is limited to the use of analogies. This limitation of our understanding is the main reason why the great world religions have used concepts like reincarnation, heaven, and hell to explain the nature of life after death. Direct access to the next world is impossible, even as a baby cannot have knowledge of the world outside the womb until after birth. Bahá'u'lláh describes the Bahá'í view of life after death as follows:

> Know thou of a truth that the soul, after its separation from the body, will continue to progress until it attaineth the presence of God, in a state and condition which neither the revolution of ages and centuries, nor the changes and chances of this world, can alter. It will endure as long as the Kingdom of God, His sovereignty, His dominion and power will endure. It will manifest the signs of God and His attributes, and will reveal His loving kindness and bounty. The movement of My Pen is stilled when it attempteth to befittingly describe the loftiness and glory of so exalted a station. The honor with which the Hand of Mercy will invest the soul is such as no tongue can adequately reveal, nor any other earthly agency describe. Blessed is the soul which, at the hour of its separation from the body, is sanctified from the vain imaginings of the peoples of the world.

Such a soul liveth and moveth in accordance with the
Will of its Creator, and entereth the all-highest Paradise. The Maids of Heaven, inmates of the loftiest
mansions, will circle around it, and the Prophets of God
and His chosen ones will seek its companionship. With
them that soul will freely converse, and will recount
unto them that which it hath been made to endure in
the path of God, the Lord of all worlds. If any man be
told that which hath been ordained for such a soul in
the worlds of God, the Lord of the throne on high and
of earth below, his whole being will instantly blaze out
in his great longing to attain that most exalted, that
sanctified and resplendent station... The nature of
the soul after death can never be described, nor is it
meet and permissible to reveal its whole character to
the eyes of men. The Prophets and Messengers of God
have been sent down for the sole purpose of guiding
mankind to the straight Path of Truth. The purpose
underlying their revelation hath been to educate all
men, that they may, at the hour of death, ascend, in the
utmost purity and sanctity and with absolute detachment, to the throne of the Most High. The light which
these souls radiate is responsible for the progress of the
world and the advancement of its peoples. They are
like unto leaven which leaveneth the world of being, and
constitute the animating force through which the arts
and wonders of the world are made manifest. Through
them the clouds rain their bounty upon men, and the
earth bringeth forth its fruits. All things must needs
have a cause, a motive power, an animating principle.
These souls and symbols of detachment have provided,
and will continue to provide, the supreme moving impulse in the world of being. The world beyond is as
different from this world as this world is different from
that of the child while still in the womb of its mother.[12]

13.7 Caste

Gandhi was ardently against untouchability, nevertheless he did believe in the philosophical framework of the caste system.* Specifically, he believed that caste was inherited:

> The Gita does talk of *varna* [caste or color] being according to *guna* [attribute or mode] and *karma* [action], but *guna* and *karma* are inherited by birth. The law of *varna* is nothing if not by birth.[13]

There is no doubt that caste was an integral part of the ancient religions of the Indian subcontinent, but Bahá'ís believe that since God alone is eternal, therefore all traditions must eventually yield to the winds of change—everything save God is subject to change. Bahá'u'lláh has stated that for this age the central principle is unity. Hence caste-based divisions—along with racial, ethnic, class, and religious divisions—must be eliminated. Indeed, divisions of caste, race, etc. can have no place in a nonviolent civilization.

---

*See also Section 6.3.

Chapter Notes

1. 'Abdu'l-Bahá, quoted in *Bahá'í World Faith: Selected Writings of Bahá'u'lláh and 'Abdu'l-Bahá* (Wilmette: Bahá'í Publishing Trust, 1971), 411–412.

2. *The Gandhi Reader: A Sourcebook of His Life and Writings*. Ed. Homer A. Jack (New York: Grove Press, 1994), 304

3. *The Light of Divine Guidance: The Messages from the Guardian of the Bahá'í Faith to the Bahá'ís of Germany and Austria* (Hofheim-Langenhain: Bahá'í-Verlag, 1982), 71

4. *The Gandhi Reader: A Sourcebook of His Life and Writings*, 306

5. *The Gospel of Selfless Action or The Gita According to Gandhi.* Ed. Mahadev Desai (Ahmedabad: Navajivan Publishing House, 1984), 262.

6. *Kitáb-i-Íqán* (Wilmette: Bahá'í Publishing Trust, 1989), 255.

7. *Kitáb-i-Íqán*, 33–43.

8. *The Gospel of Selfless Action or The Gita According to Gandhi*, 264.

9. *The Gospel of Selfless Action or The Gita According to Gandhi*, 127–128.

10. *Kitáb-i-Íqán*, 49–158.

11. The *Upanishads* contain the highest form of philosophical introspection in Hinduism and and are seen as perennial sources of spiritual knowledge. The *Upanishads* more clearly set forth the prime Vedic doctrines like Self-realization, yoga and meditation, karma and reincarnation, which were hidden or kept veiled under the symbols of the older religion. The older *Upanishads* are usually affixed to a particular *Veda,* but the more recent ones are not. It is believed by many people that the *Upanishads* became prevalent some centuries before the time of Krishna and Buddha. The *Kaushitaki* is an early *Upanishad* that is considered to be among the more important.

12. Bahá'u'lláh, quoted in J. E. Esslemont, *Bahá'u'lláh and the New Era,* 5th rev. ed. (Wilmette: Bahá'í Publishing Trust, 1987), 102.

13. M. K. Gandhi, *Young India,* 24 November 1927.

Chapter 14

Epilogue

14.1   The Role of the Individual

This book has attempted to study various aspects of a nonviolent, spiritual civilization of the future, as envisaged by Gandhi and by the Bahá'ís. Thus far, however, the role of the individual in this future civilization has not been discussed at length. It is conceivable that if the very structure of civilization suffers drastic change, then the nature of the constituent individuals cannot remain unaffected.

It is even possible that the very conceptions of individuality and of self will be forced to undergo a reformulation. In today's society, people think of themselves as being essentially separate from others and as having distinct identities. We often use words like "I" and "mine" to describe ourselves. This way of thinking about our selves forces a certain sense of separation and division between the individual and the social organism we constitute. However, this concept of "I" is only an idealistic approximation—like Euclid's definition of a point—because we are at all times "connected" to others and to the universe by spiritual as well as material forces. The time may very well come when the concept of an isolated, point-like "self" must be abandoned.[1] It could be argued that the concept of "I" and of self has been the cause of much sorrow, complacency, and ignorance. Minds infected with this concept can become obsessed with "self-interest," "self-esteem," "self-image," and even succomb to prejudices based on "my race," "my religion," "my country," etc.

In contrast, people who focus their minds on selfless service to humanity inevitably experience the boundless, unconditional happiness that characterizes self-transcendence. In such a condition, individuals can begin to seek fulfilment in the "divine good pleasure" rather than in their own. Freed thus from "selfish" desire, they attune their hearts instead to the true Object of Desire, the Ancient Beauty. References to variations of this theme abound in Gandhian and Bahá'í literature. Bahá'u'lláh writes:

> Let your vision be world-embracing, rather than confined to your own self.[2]

> O My Servant! Free thyself from the fetters of this world, and loose thy soul from the prison of self . Seize thy chance, for it will come to thee no more.[3]

> The death of self is needed here, not rhetoric: Be nothing, then, and walk upon the waves.[4]

'Abdu'l-Bahá writes:

> A Persian king was one night in his palace, living in the greatest luxury and comfort. Through excessive joy and gladness he addressed a certain man, saying: "Of all my life this is the happiest moment. Praise be to God, from every point prosperity appears and fortune smiles! My treasury is full and the army is well taken care of. My palaces are many; my land unlimited; my family is well off; my honor and sovereignty are great. What more could I want!" The poor man at the gate of his palace spoke out, saying: "O kind king! Assuming that you are from every point of view so happy, free from every worry and sadness—do you not worry for us? You say that on your own account you have no worries—but do you never worry about the poor in your land? Is it becoming or meet that you should be so well off and we in such dire want and need? In view of our needs and troubles how can you rest in your palace,

how can you even say that you are free from worries
and sorrows? As a ruler you must not be so egoistic as
to think of yourself alone but you must think of those
who are your subjects. When we are comfortable then
you will be comfortable; when we are in misery how can
you, as a king, be in happiness?" The purport is this
that we are all inhabiting one globe of earth. In reality
we are one family and each one of us is a member of
this family. We must all be in the greatest happiness
and comfort, under a just rule and regulation which is
according to the good pleasure of God, thus causing us
to be happy, for this life is fleeting.[5]

He who has reached the state of self-sacrifice has true
joy. Temporal joy will vanish.[6]

Gandhi writes:

Not until we have reduced ourselves to nothingness can
we conquer the evil in us. God demands nothing less
than complete self-surrender as the price for the only
real freedom that is worth having. And when a man
thus loses himself he immediately finds himself in the
service of all that lives. It becomes his delight and
recreation. He is a new man, never weary of spending
himself in the service of God's creation.[7]

14.2 Prospects: From Self to Service

If self-forgetfulness is the secret of happiness and true freedom,
then we can expect that, with time, humankind will outgrow the
obsession with the egocentric concepts of "I" and "mine," etc. Indeed, a nonviolent civilization can only be built upon the foundation of self-sacrificing individuals, certainly not egocentric and
arrogant people. It may take centuries for such drastic changes to
take full effect, since it necessarily involves altering the very structure of language, the way we think, old habits and traditions, etc.
But there are many reasons to bet that such changes must eventually come. Just as infants slowly become less self-centered as they

develop into adults, similarly humankind will give less importance to "selfishness" and focus more on service. Regarding the path of sacrifice that leads from self to service, 'Abdu'l-Bahá writes:

> Until a being setteth his foot in the plane of sacrifice, he is bereft of every favour and grace; and this plane of sacrifice is the realm of dying to the self, that the radiance of the living God may then shine forth. The martyr's field is the place of detachment from self, that the anthems of eternity may be upraised. Do all ye can to become wholly weary of self, and bind yourselves to that Countenance of Splendours; and once ye have reached such heights of servitude, ye will find, gathered within your shadow, all created things. This is bound-less grace; this is the highest sovereignty; this is the life that dieth not. All else save this is at the last but manifest perdition and great loss...
>
> Let us, like candles, burn away; as moths, let us scorch our wings; as the field larks, vent our plaintive cries; as the nightingales, burst forth in lamentations. Even as the clouds let us shed down tears, and as the lightning flashes let us laugh at our coursings through east and west. By day, by night, let us think but of spreading the sweet savours of God. Let us not keep on forever with our fancies and illusions, with our analysing and interpreting and circulating of complex dubieties. Let us put aside all thoughts of self; let us close our eyes to all on earth, let us neither make known our suffer-ings nor complain of our wrongs. Rather let us become oblivious of our own selves, and drinking down the wine of heavenly grace, let us cry out our joy, and lose our-selves in the beauty of the All-Glorious.[8]

Gandhi shared similar views:

> ... it is no non-violence if we merely love those that love us. It is non-violence only when we love those that hate us.[9]

So long as man remains selfish and does not care for

the happiness of others, he is no better than an animal and perhaps worse. His superiority to the animal is seen only when we find him caring for his family. He is still more human, that is, much higher than the animal, when he extends his concept of the family to include his country or community as well. He climbs still higher in the scale when he comes to regard the human race as his family. A man is an animal or imperfect to the extent that he falls behind in his service to humanity.[10]

If we could erase the 'I's' and 'Mine's' from religion, politics, economics, etc., we shall soon be free and bring heaven upon earth.[11]

It may be challenging to understand the nature of what is being asked of us. After all, the path of sacrifice that leads from the valleys of self towards the heights of service very much remains the road less traveled, the straight and narrow path. Nevertheless, the underlying concept is simple enough: to think less of ourselves and more of others. Certainly, it is not a new concept. How well has it been eloquently explained in ages past, by such as John Donne (1572–1631):

No man is an island, entire of itself;
every man is a piece of the continent, a part of the main;
if a clod be washed away by the sea,
Europe is the less, as well as if a promontory were,
as well as if a manor of thy friend's or of thine own were;
any man's death diminishes me,
because I am involved in mankind;
and therefore never send to know for whom the bell tolls;
it tolls for thee...

* * * * *

Please God, as we advance in forgetting ourselves in service to humanity, we will blossom into radiant spirits, and a new, nonviolent civilization will effloresce.

194 CHAPTER 14. EPILOGUE

Chapter Notes

1. Consider, for example, the sentence "this book belongs to me" in comparison to another sentence, "this book belongs to you," spoken towards someone else. In the first case, there is an underlying sense of selfishness because the ownership of the book is implicitly being denied to the other person. In the second case, no such selfishness is apparent, but rather only a sense of unselfish, expansive generosity. Moreover, the description of our selves using the age-old concepts of "I" and "mine" is inherently distorted by an artificial sense of separation between the "us" and "them." The first person of the singular implies a primacy that, while suited perfectly to the description of the Oneness of God, nevertheless oversimplifies the complex web of relations that relate "us" to "our" world. Indeed, the very thought of "I" and "mine" are inextricably linked to self-centeredness. No such problem seems apparent in the use of the second and third persons of the singular or plural, because there is no implication of primacy.

2. *Gleanings from the Writings of Bahá'u'lláh*. Trans. Shoghi Effendi (Wilmette: Bahá'í Publishing Trust, 1976), 94.

3. *The Hidden Words of Bahá'u'lláh*. Trans. Shoghi Effendi (Wilmette: Bahá'í Publishing Trust, 1985), 36.

4. *The Seven Valleys and the Four Valleys* (Wilmette: Bahá'í Publishing Trust, 1991), 52.

5. *Foundations of World Unity* (Wilmette: Bahá'í Publishing Trust, 1979), 41–42.

6. *Paris Talks: Addresses given by 'Abdu'l-Bahá in Paris in 1911–1912* (London: Bahá'í Publishing Trust, 1972), 179.

7. *All Men Are Brothers*, 68.

8. *Selections from the Writings of 'Abdu'l-Bahá* (Haifa: Bahá'í World Centre, 1978), pp. 76–77, 179–180, 236–237.

9. *All Men Are Brothers: Life and Thoughts of Mahatma Gandhi as Told in His Own Words*. Ed. K Kripalani (Paris: UNESCO, 1969), 86.

10. *The Selected Works of Mahatma Gandhi: Volume Four (the Basic Works)*. Ed. Shriman Narayan (Ahmedabad: Navajivan Publishing House, 1968), 29.

11. *The Essential Writings of Mahatma Gandhi*. Ed. Raghavan Iyer (Oxford: Oxford University Press, 1990), 414.

Bibliography

'Abdu'l-Bahá in London: Addresses, and Notes of Conversations. (London: Bahá'í Publishing Trust, 1982).

All Men Are Brothers: Life and Thoughts of Mahatma Gandhi as Told in His Own Words. Ed. K Kripalani (Paris: UNESCO, 1969).

Bahá'í Administration, Shoghi Effendi (Wilmette: Bahá'í Publishing Trust, 1974).

Bahá'í Social and Economic Development Activities: 1996–1997, Prepared by the Office of Social and Economic Development, Bahá'í World Centre, Haifa.

Bahá'í World Faith: Selected Writings of Bahá'u'lláh and 'Abdu'l-Bahá (Wilmette: Bahá'í Publishing Trust, 1971).

Bahá'u'lláh, A statement prepared by the Bahá'í International Community's Office of Public Information on the occasion of the centenary of Bahá'u'lláh's passing.

Bahá'u'lláh and the New Era, J. E. Esslemont (Wilmette: Bahá'í Publishing Trust, 1976).

Bahá'u'lláh and the New Era, J. E. Esslemont, 5th rev. ed. (Wilmette: Bahá'í Publishing Trust, 1987).

The Collected Works of Mahatma Gandhi (New Delhi: Navajivan, 1958–84).

A Compilation on Bahá'í Education Compiled by the Research Department of the Universal House of Justice (Haifa: Bahá'í

World Centre, 1976).

Discovery of India, Jawaharlal Nehru (London: Meridian Books, 1960).

The Essential Writings of Mahatma Gandhi. Ed. Raghavan Iyer (Oxford: Oxford University Press, 1990).

Foundations of World Unity (Wilmette: Bahá'í Publishing Trust, 1979).

Gandhi the Man, Eknath Easwaran (Petaluma: Nilgiri Press, 1983).

The Gandhi Reader: A Sourcebook of His Life and Writings. Ed. Homer A. Jack (New York: Grove Press, 1994).

Gleanings from the Writings of Bahá'u'lláh. Trans. Shoghi Effendi (Wilmette: Bahá'í Publishing Trust, 1976).

God Passes By, Shoghi Effendi (Wilmette: Bahá'í Publishing Trust, 1987).

The Gospel of Selfless Action or The Gita According to Gandhi. Ed. Mahadev Desai (Ahmedabad: Navajivan Publishing House, 1984).

The Hidden Words of Bahá'u'lláh. Trans. Shoghi Effendi (Wilmette: Bahá'í Publishing Trust, 1985).

Hindu Dharma (New Delhi: Orient Paperbacks, 1987).

In Search of the Supreme Ed. V. B. Kher (Ahmedabad: Navajivan press, 1962).

Kitáb-i-Aqdas (Haifa: Bahá'í World Centre, 1992).

Kitáb-i-Íqán (Wilmette: Bahá'í Publishing Trust, 1989).

The Light of Divine Guidance, Shoghi Effendi (Hofheim-Langenhain: Bahá'í-Verlag, 1982).

Lights of Guidance: A Bahá'í Reference File, 2nd Edition. Ed. Helen Hornby (New Delhi: Bahá'í Publishing Trust, 1988).

The Mind of Mahatma Gandhi. Ed. R. K. Prabhu and U. R. Rao (Ahmedabad: Navajivan Publishing House, 1967).

The Moral and Political Writings of Mahatma Gandhi. Ed. Raghavan Iyer (Oxford: Oxford University Press, 1986).

The Overworked American: The Unexpected Decline of Leisure, J. B. Schor (New York: Basic Books, 1991).

Paris Talks: Addresses given by 'Abdu'l-Bahá in Paris in 1911–1912 (London: Bahá'í Publishing Trust, 1972).

Philosophy: A Text with Readings, 6th ed., M. Velasquez (Belmont: Wadsworth Publishing Company, 1997).

Prayers and Meditations by Bahá'u'lláh. Trans. Shoghi Effendi (Wilmette: Bahá'í Publishing Trust, 1987).

The Proclamation of Bahá'u'lláh (Wilmette: Bahá'í Publishing Trust, 1978).

The Promise of World Peace. A statement of the Universal House of Justice addressed to the peoples of the world, dated October 1985.

The Promulgation of Universal Peace: Talks Delivered by 'Abdu'l-Bahá during His Visit to the United States and Canada in 1912 (Wilmette: Bahá'í Publishing Trust, 1982).

The Prosperity Of Humankind, A statement prepared in 1995 by the Bahá'í International Community's Office of Public Information.

The Selected Works of Mahatma Gandhi. Ed. Shriman Narayan (Ahmedabad: Navajivan Publishing House, 1968).

Selections from the Writings of 'Abdu'l-Bahá (Haifa: Bahá'í World Centre, 1978).

Selections from the Writings of the Báb (Haifa: Bahá'í World Centre, 1982).

The Seven Valleys and the Four Valleys (Wilmette: Bahá'í Publishing Trust, 1991).

Some Answered Questions (Wilmette: Bahá'í Publishing Trust, 1990).

Tablets of 'Abdu'l-Bahá (Chicago: Bahá'í Publishing Society, 1908).

Tablets of Bahá'u'lláh Revealed after the Kitáb-i-Aqdas (Wilmette: Bahá'í Publishing Trust, 1988).

Timeless Healing: The Power and Biology of Belief, Herbert Benson (New York: Scribner, 1996).

The World Order of Bahá'u'lláh, Shoghi Effendi (Wilmette: Bahá'í Publishing Trust, 1991).

Young India, M. K. Gandhi.

Index